THE Ultimate Bath

Mary Wynn Ryan

Consultant:
John Spitz, CKD, CBD, ASID

Photo Consultant:
Barbara H. Jacksier

Publications International, Ltd.

Mary Wynn Ryan is the author of Publications International's *The Ultimate Kitchen* and has written about home furnishings and interior design for numerous publications, including *Woman's Day Decorating Ideas* magazine. She has served as Midwest editor of *Design Times* magazine and was director of consumer and trade marketing for the Chicago Merchandise Mart's residential design center, which included kitchen and bath products. She is president of Winning Ways Marketing, an editorial and marketing consulting firm that specializes in home design and decorating.

John Spitz, CKD, CBD, ASID, is the director of professional programs for the National Kitchen & Bath Association (NKBA), the trade association that sets the benchmark for professional development and certification in the kitchen and bath industry. Prior to joining NKBA's staff, he owned and operated Dreamscape Designs, a firm that specialized in kitchen and bath design. In addition to earning his Certified Bathroom Designer (CBD), Certified Kitchen Designer (CKD), and National Council for Interior Design Qualification (NCIDQ) certifications, he has received numerous design awards, including a first-place award in NKBA's 1990 Design Competition.

Barbara H. Jacksier is an editor, a consultant, and a frequent guest lecturer on home design topics. She is the editor of several decorating magazines for Harris Publications, including *Country Decorating* magazine's *Country Kitchens, Bedrooms & Baths* and *Country Collectibles*.

Louis Weber, CEO
Publications International, Ltd.
7373 North Cicero Avenue
Lincolnwood, Illinois 60712

Permission is never granted for commercial purposes.

Manufactured in China.

8 7 6 5 4 3 2 1

ISBN: 0-7853-4464-0

Library of Congress Card Number: 00-112194

Contents

Planning Your Dream Bath

IT MAY BE the smallest room in the house, but the impact of a wonderful new bathroom can be enormous. Inch for inch, simply no other home improvement yields more convenience and personal pampering. Are you dreaming of a lavish master bath? A safe, fun bath to be shared by your teen and toddler? An accessible, pretty bath for your mom? A powder room you can be proud of? Start your planning right here. Browse this book for savvy questions to ask, innovative products to choose, and beautiful designs to inspire you. From clever facelifts that knock off decades to a totally new bathroom where none was before, you'll see a world of fresh designs you can adapt to create the new bath you've been waiting for.

What makes a glorious master bath? A vista framed by a classically arched doorway leading to a private toilet compartment, a magnificent tub, and other amenities in a luxurious space embellished by elegant woods, marble, and mirrors.

AMERICA IS A bath-happy country. Like our Puritan forebears, we still associate cleanliness with virtue, but today, we also associate it with hedonistic pampering. From the skimpy, sanitary, one-per-household white box of the 1950s, the bath has blossomed into a beckoning retreat. While not every bath can be the statement-making, opulent type made popular in the ornate '80s, every bath can benefit from the flow of great new ideas entering the market. Even baths that can't be enlarged are looking and feeling much better these days, thanks to inventive fixtures, attractive personal touches, appealing color schemes, and intelligent design.

Does your bath need a facelift? Take a cue from this bath, which features a handsome corner sink with a furniture-grade wood base and a marble top. The recessed triple medicine cabinet is in character with the sink; together they create a focal point that elevates this full bath to designer status.

Creating a better bath isn't just an indulgence; it's a smart idea. One of the best home improvement investments you can make is adding a second full bath to a one-bath house or remodeling an existing bath. On average, you'll recoup a bit over 70 percent of your cost at resale time. Adding a first-floor powder room offers a good payback, too. Where once a single bathroom for a family of six or eight was acceptable, today "enough" baths to many home buyers means one for every two people plus a powder room.

Even if you don't plan to sell your house soon, a new or remodeled bath can make a huge improvement in your family's quality of life, day in and day out. A new bath can relieve squabbles over morning congestion, and a remodeled one can add a whole new dimension of comfort. Even a relatively simple replacement or redecoration project can add valuable safety measures and refresh your spirits. Start thinking now about what would make a real difference to your quality of life.

WHAT MATTERS MOST TO YOU?

This book will show you exciting baths of various sizes, configurations, and styles, but they're only a starting point for your own planning. Before you plunge into your project, think carefully about what you like and dislike about your present bathroom. Do you need more space in the master bath or just a savvier floor plan that lets two people share the room more comfortably? Is there enough counterspace and storage

space? Are you tired of the outdated color scheme you've lived with since you moved in? Do you want all new fixtures or just a whirlpool in place of your old tub? Do you crave a bath you don't have to share with the kids or long for a drop-dead powder room or guest bath?

Sit down with family members, and get specific about what current problems you want the new bathroom to solve. Even young children can have good insights, and the more involved everyone is, the more they'll buy into the process.

Once you have an idea of what you want to change, start identifying solutions that appeal to you. Look through home design and decorating books and magazines, and tag or photocopy pages showing bathroom designs and products you like. Then start a scrapbook of ideas, photos, and product catalogs that will help the professionals you hire understand your tastes and needs. You can also gather ideas by visiting the many Web sites that offer bath design products or by spending some time "just looking" in the local bath design center

Behind these beguiling, French country–inspired cabinet doors is a wealth of clever storage to meet everyone's needs, including hidden laundry baskets, makeup trays, and a pull-out/swivel TV platform. Designer: Sally Ann Sullivan, CKD, Showcase Kitchens and Baths, Inc. Cabinets: Wm Ohs, Inc.

If your bath is in need of more counterspace, don't assume you have to use up an entire wall with a long countertop. This bath features a uniquely angled custom vanity top, offering plenty of counterspace as well as extra visual excitement. Designers: Joe McDermott and Diane Wandmaker, CKD, Kitchen Studio. Manufacturer: Crestwood.

or department of your nearby home improvement store.

Unless you're planning the very simplest redecoration, you'll want to talk to bath design professionals about what you need and want. When interviewing them, be prepared to answer a lot of questions about how you and your family live and how you'll use the space. Use your scrapbook to identify for the professional what styles you like: You'd be surprised by what "traditional" means to different people!

The more carefully you've done your homework, the more it will pay off when you actually sit down to discuss your needs with a bath specialist. Keep an open mind if your answers lead the designer to suggest something unexpected. It may be the perfect solution for you, your family, and your home.

A master bath suite is a luxury that's well worth the effort if your home's layout will allow for it. Here, a pair of half-round vanity cabinets flanks a curved doorway to create a symphony of pleasing, repeated forms as well as a symmetrical balance that is both restful and impressive.

B$_{ATH}$ DESIGN and construction come under five major categories. In pursuit of the ultimate bath, find the one that's right for you.

NEW CONSTRUCTION

New construction refers to work done on a house that's being entirely built from the ground up. If you're building from scratch, you've got the most leeway in creating the bath size, location, and configuration you want. With new construction, it's easy to fit a master bath within your master bedroom suite and a bath between or near your children's bedrooms. You can specify a half bath or a powder room near the dining room, living room, or family room—whatever seems best to you. And if you want another bath in your home office or guest suite, above the garage in the bonus room, or downstairs in the rec room, you can have that, too.

Of course, your overall house and lot size will affect the size and number of bathrooms you can fit in, and your budget for baths is just one part of your home-building dollars. But in new construction, you can trade off square feet and dollars between the bathrooms and other spaces for maximum flexibility.

REMODELING

Remodeling involves major changes that may take your bathroom in a whole new direction. Remodeling is what you're up to if you need to change the whole "footprint" (i.e., configuration and size) of

This bath fits in a wealth of comforts, including a steam shower with a built-in seat, a sauna, a separate toilet compartment, and a wall niche that houses towels with a towel warmer below.
Designer: John A. Buscarello, ASID. Manufacturer: Wood-Mode.

your bathroom to add space or to reshape the room for better access. This often involves relocating (not just replacing) fixtures and their accompanying water supply and drain/waste/vent pipes, moving doors and windows, and maybe even taking space from nearby closets or small bedrooms.

While your existing home's size and layout will affect how radically you can change your bathrooms, you can make surprisingly big changes. Remodeling doesn't have to depend on what your old bathroom looked like, only on what your needs and wishes are and what your budget dictates. If you need help with more than one bathroom, you may want to plan them as one project. At the same time you create a sumptuous private bath for you and your spouse, you may be able to add a roomy, safe second bath for your kids down the hall. If you love your property and your neighborhood, remodeling can let you love your bathrooms, too!

RENOVATION

Renovation involves significant changes while remaining faithful to the spirit and overall look of your existing house. Renovation is appropriate if your home's "bones" are good and if you like its style in general. If your home is historically significant, you may be required to handle any upgrades with great respect for the existing style and structure. Since bathrooms have changed much more radically over the past century than, say, bedrooms, renovation's challenge is to preserve the best of the past while giving you comfortable, workable baths for today's lifestyle.

Bathrooms have always been pretty skimpy affairs. However, many pre-World War II houses have an abundance of little bedrooms, and annex-

ing one could give you the space you need. There's also an abundant supply of vintage-looking fixtures and fittings to give your bath nostalgic style with modern performance.

REPLACEMENT

Replacement, or "changeout," means taking out one or more of your old fixtures and installing new ones in exactly the same places. Since most of the typical bath is taken up by fixtures, replacing dated pieces will make a dramatic improvement in your bath's look and function. Replacing fixtures will naturally give you a more attractive, better-performing bath, but it won't address big problems, such as lack of floor space or storage, inconvenient

Striking and chic, this bath owes a lot of its modern pizzazz to new fixtures like this chrome-legged sink and gooseneck faucet. A no-frills mirror and wall-hung cabinet are other easy changes that make a big impact.

access, or a poor location within the house. Keep in mind that, depending on how much your new fixtures' profiles differ from the old ones, you may have to repair or replace wallcoverings, tile, flooring, and molding in surrounding areas. For this reason, many people plan a replacement and redecoration project together. On the plus side, if you plan a simple replacement of fixtures, you may not need a building permit and can probably find a competent handyperson to take care of the job.

Obviously, swapping an old wall-hung sink for a new similarly scaled pedestal sink is going to be a lot easier and less messy than replacing an old built-in bathtub with a new one, so be sure to match the scope of the job with the skill and experience of the worker. And don't forget that replacement can mean leaving the old tiled-in sink and tub intact but putting in beautiful new fittings (e.g., faucets, pop-up drains, etc.) or trading tacky old light fixtures for attractive new ones. These small improvements can make a big difference!

REDECORATION

Redecoration involves sprucing up without all the tearing down. It's cheaper and easier than remodeling or renovation, but depending on what you have done, it can cost a lot less than, or as much as, replacing all the fixtures. If your bathroom basically suits you as it is, but you'd like a fresher, more fashionable appearance, redecoration may be just what you need.

Designer showhouses sponsored by local charities are especially good places to see bath redecorations, as designers seldom spring for new fixtures or wall and floor surfaces. Instead, they splurge on inventive or glorious wallcoverings or faux-finish

New wallcoverings and borders can refresh the look of any bath. Here, watercolor stripes and stylized wave motifs create chic transitional style and visually enlarge the space. Wallcoverings: Seabrook Wallcoverings, Inc.

paint jobs; exciting window treatments, shower curtains, and towels; and fresh accessories that carry the room's decorating theme. If you're tired of your tile walls, laminate vanity top, or knotty pine sink cabinet, your hardware store has special products that you can use to repaint them to coordinate with your newly painted or papered upper walls. You can even refinish your old bathtub with hardware store products that are similar to nail polish. Meticulous preparation of these surfaces is critical, but these treatments are an economical way to improve the look of your bath, fast.

Whatever you choose, be sure your expectations are in line with what's possible, given the scope of the work and your budget. Veteran homeowners who've been through any of these productions agree: Even the ultimate bath is only a small part of your life, so keep things in perspective.

Great Results on Any Budget

INCH FOR INCH, the bathroom is the most expensive room in the house to remodel, largely because of the variety of skilled labor required from plumbing and electrical contractors, carpenters, and other experts. Materials, too, take their toll in cost. So, heed some advice from the experts and from families who've done the job already: Take your time at the beginning to make sure each decision reflects your tastes and meets your needs. You don't want your bathroom project to be a financial burden, so make sure you really need the high-end solution in each case, and plan as much as possible in advance to avoid costly changes in the middle of the project.

To ensure you won't lop off something essential when you fall in love with a "nice-to-have" item in the showrooms, make a list of everything you'd love to have in your new bath. Now, divide this list into A) things you really need and B) things you want but could live without for now. As you shop and plan, make a note of the nice-to-have items you find, but don't commit to them until you've finalized the essentials and added up the costs.

Try to anticipate what features can easily be added and what can't. One good example: You'll want to install reinforcements for a grab bar before you tile the walls, even if you don't need the bar now, but you can decide to add a towel ring at any time, since it doesn't need reinforcement.

In general, it's wise to get the floor plan and any back-of-the-wall structural needs accounted for first. You can get a faux-marble laminate or a cultured marble vanity countertop now and replace it with a genuine marble slab later, but if the sink's in the wrong place, you still won't be happy.

What makes up the costs of a new bathroom? Most costs fall under the broad heading of time (actual person-hours, or labor) and materials, sometimes abbreviated on proposals as "T&M." You can save money on both.

SAVE MONEY ON LABOR

In construction, time is expressed as hourly rates paid to various workers on your project. Invest your time instead of theirs, and you'll save big.

Most homeowners find it's best to do their part before and after the workers do theirs, instead of trying to work at the same time. For example, you could steam off wallpaper, pull up old flooring, and remove old fixtures before the workers arrive. But use common sense: Be sure you know how and where to shut off water pipes before pulling out fixtures, and find out where wiring and pipes are located before you tear out walls. Steer clear of removing old insulation that may contain asbestos or old paint that may contain lead. And if your home has historical significance, get guidance from an expert before tackling anything. You don't want to disturb something of value.

Before you start the project, discuss with your contractor what you're willing to tackle, and work out specifically what you'll do and what they'll do. Then, get that agreement into the written contract, and make sure they deduct the cost of your work from their bid.

When it's time to put on the finishing touches, you can paint the walls, screw on switchplates, and, yes, pick up the debris rather than paying someone else to do it. The money you save on labor can pay for some of those luxurious material upgrades you crave!

SAVE MONEY ON MATERIALS

Of course you'd love a marble vanity countertop; state-of-the-art imported fixtures; hand-painted wall and floor tiles; and custom vanity and storage cabinets in high-end, furniture-grade woods. If, like most of us, you can't afford them all, choose the ones that matter most to you—and find artful substitutes for the rest. A few examples:

- **High-end fixtures and fittings.** You can't turn a standard tub into a whirlpool for four or make a gravity-assist toilet work like a pressure-assist model, but you can find fixtures that mimic the look of costlier designs. Traditionally styled fixtures and fittings are widely available at all price points, so look carefully at the high-priced models, and then seek out the more affordable looks in the same general style. Contemporary innovations, such as one-piece elongated-bowl toilets, are harder to replicate at modest prices, but you can skimp elsewhere if you can't do without them.

- **Marble vanity countertops.** Marble slabs are the top-of-the-line choice, but as with diamonds, it's finding one large, intact piece that's so costly. You can get the same look for less if you opt for large marble tiles set flush to each other. For even less, you can choose "cultured" marble, which is marble dust bonded into a solid slab, or, for still less, select a laminate countertop with a faux-marble pattern.

- **Handmade, custom-colored, imported ceramic wall tiles.** If they're too costly to use throughout, use them as "bath jewelry" in tile borders and accents. Choose a compatible plain tile for most of the installation, and save the custom pieces for eye-

Beautiful custom ceramic tiles are like jewelry for your bath: Use them to spice up more economical plain tiles and to accent your design theme.
Designer: Kim Bernard, ASID, Walker Zanger.
Tiles: Walker Zanger.

level areas such as the backsplash or a border around a window.

- **Luxury flooring.** Marble flooring may be out of reach, but ceramic tiles with a faux-marble look or handsome vinyl flooring are good-looking, affordable alternatives.

- **Custom cabinetry.** Many vanity and storage cabinets come in such a wide array of stock sizes and shapes that they assure a virtually custom fit, so use stock cabinets wherever you can. If your budget says pine or oak but your heart says cherry or maple, you may prefer to paint rather than stain your cabinets to disguise the more prominent grains of the lower-cost woods. To create a custom look, replace ho-hum hardware with novelty cabinet door pulls such as pewter fish, whitewashed or verdigris brass shells, or flower-painted porcelain.

- **Fancy faux finishes.** Bathrooms are a great place to indulge your desire for a hand-painted tromp l'oeil garden scene or a beautiful ragged or marbled faux finish, but the cost can be high for a professional artist's time. Look into do-it-yourself stenciling and faux-finish kits available in most craft, hobby, and paint stores, or see if your local school's art department boasts any great student portfolios. Another option is wallcovering that gives the look for less.

Bottom line: Whatever the look you like, you can probably find similar looks within your budget. When in doubt, remember that the rich look is to spend on function and keep style beautifully simple.

PLANNING FOR RESALE VALUE

You want your new bath to meet your needs and reflect your tastes—right up until the day you want to put your house on the market. That's when you'll be glad if you kept an eye on what the average home buyer in your price range is looking for. A consumer-pleasing bathroom is one of the top home-selling elements, but even an opulent, custom bath can detract if it's too individualistic. Appropriate upgrades can return as much as 70 to 90 percent or more of their cost to you at resale time, making it much easier to get your asking price on the home. When making decisions about materials, keep these tips in mind:

- Upgrades to better-performing basic fixtures or windows, for example, almost always add to both the sales appeal and the value of your home. Plain stock ceramic tile will hold its beauty and its value longer than laminate for about the same price, and a simple porcelain sink bowl has more timeless appeal than its cultured marble cousin in the same price range.

- Don't go beyond what's typical for new or improved baths in your home's price range. Experts advise not to spend more than 10 percent, tops, of your home's current market value on a

This industrial modern loft-style bath needed visual anchoring. It got a warm, substantial boost from the natural wood vanity; slate-look counter; drop-in porcelain sinks; and traditional, brushed-finish drawer pulls and sink fittings.

bath improvement. A palatial bath in a cute little house will make your home less, not more, desirable. You'd be much better off putting in a second full bath if you don't have one or adding a powder room or half bath if you do.

- When it comes to flooring, countertops, and other installed products that are available in many colors and patterns, think twice before making a strong fashion statement with these areas. You don't want to date your bathroom or turn off your best home-buying prospects in a few years.

- Keep it simple when it comes to sinks, faucets, and other fixtures and fittings. If you're tired of shiny chrome, look for brushed pewter or chrome and brass, but keep the style free of curlicues or other design elements that can be dated-looking or hard to clean.

- Choose neutral colors for installed products, especially if they are not luxury-grade. Midtone neutrals show wear the least; light-colored neutrals give a spacious, bright feeling. Be a bit careful of black, chocolate, or other dark colors: They disguise grime just fine but show soap scum, hard-water stains, and some marring worse than lighter tones.

- Do you crave an adventurous scheme? Indulge your love of bright colors or patterns in wallcoverings (paint plus

Keeping fixtures and built-in shelving white gives this modern loft-style bath plenty of room for expression in the accent pieces and wall color. Green ceramic mugs on the open shelves hold small bath necessities in style. A simple wood-frame mirror is green today but can be given a new color when the owner changes the wall paint.

A universal-design-savvy bath like this one is safe and comfortable for people of varying ages and physical abilities—important if you want to stay in your home as you age or if family members have special needs.

contrasting color tiles to make the edge more visible, increasing aisle width from 36 to 40 inches, or specifying no-scald faucets and wing-style faucet handles that don't require wrist-twisting, can make a significant difference in your bath's long-term usefulness. If a family member has allergies or you want to be particularly rigorous about ecological issues, you can even specify products made with special hypoallergenic finishes and glues. If your floor plan allows, you may want to consider converting a first-floor powder room into a universally accessible full bath now.

borders are easiest to change), towels, soap dishes, guest soaps, nonslip rugs, and accessories. Wine and hunter green against bone is a whole different look than peach and turquoise blue against bone!

WHAT IF YOU'RE NOT MOVING?

Do you have young children or grandchildren? Want to stay in your home as long as possible as you age? Do you have any kind of physical limitation? "Universal design" is something you definitely want to consider for your new bath. It goes way beyond designing walkways to accommodate wheelchairs. Universal design creates a space that works for every family member at every stage of life. Something as simple as bordering a counter in

LET'S GO SHOPPING!

Before you hire the pros, spend some time looking at bath design solutions and products on the Web, in your local home improvement store's bath center, and in home decorating and remodeling books and magazines. You want to get an idea of what's available and what everything will cost, especially if you've never bought bath fixtures or haven't done so for many years. Educate yourself ahead of time, and you'll avoid "sticker shock," enjoy a better relationship with your bath professionals, and have a greater chance of getting exactly what you want.

EXPENSIVE MATERIALS and high-end fixtures won't mean anything if the bath doesn't function comfortably and safely. Even if you're just replacing old fixtures with new ones in the same place, you want installers who demonstrate that they are very familiar with building codes and the plumbing, wiring, and structural aspects of the job. Mistakes in this room can be costly or even deadly, especially with the combination of electricity and water. Moving a waste stack or a load-bearing wall is nothing to fool around with, either, so choose your bath designer and installer wisely.

You have a number of options when it comes to selecting the professional who will create your new bath, including an architect, an interior designer, or a building/remodeling contractor. If your bath is part of a whole new house or a major remodeling, all of these experts may be involved. These pros buy fixtures and other materials from a variety of sources at wholesale and charge you the retail markup, usually in addition to a professional fee for the overall planning and supervision of the work.

Hiring licensed professionals is important: If they don't apply for permits or don't do the work according to code, an inspection by building code officials could be a bad experience for you. If inspectors can't check your wiring and plumbing, you'll be compelled to tear out new drywall and fixtures so they can. Any violations will be your problem and your cost, and if anyone is injured on your premises later due to noncode installations, you'll be in trouble again. For this reason, experts advise that your contract specify that the hired professional apply for the contract in his or her name,

not yours. That way, the contractor is responsible for making sure all work is done to code. Even if you're planning to do much of the work yourself, apply for all required permits, make sure you and everyone else's work meets code, and cooperate with inspections at each stage. They exist for your protection.

For any structural work, you'll need a licensed architect or designer/builder as well as licensed contractors and skilled tradespeople. You can also work directly with a bath dealer who's most often a kitchen dealer, too. Whether this dealer is a high-end specialist or from the kitchen and bath department of your local hardware megastore, the dealer sells fixtures from his or her own showroom as well as installs them. In this case, design services to actually plan your bathroom may either be handled as a separate professional fee or built into the price of the products used in your bath. (Think twice about using dealers who advertise "free design services": If it's true, they may not be around long, or the quality may not be what you expect. If the design service price is actually built into the price of the products they install for you, you'd rather know that up front, too.)

Some bath designers are specialists but not dealers. These independent designers can spec (short for "specify," or select on your behalf) products from many sources, but they do specialize in bath design (and often kitchen design as well), offering their design services for a fee or a fee plus a markup. They may be interior designers who have decided to specialize in kitchen and bath work or dealers who no longer want to run a product showroom. Follow the same procedures as above before making your

These homeowners clearly had a specific goal in mind for this remodeling job: more storage! The result is an ultramodern bath with cabinets built right up to the ceiling to make use of every square inch of space.

mechanical, and building, among others, as well as design principles, drawing techniques, construction estimating, and more.

Some designers charge a fee plus a markup on products they specify; others take only a consulting fee. Most design providers will ask for a retainer (i.e., a percentage of the projected design cost) in advance.

Whomever you choose, he or she may provide only the design plus consultations with you and your tradespeople. Or they may oversee the contractors who, in turn, will supervise subcontractors such as the tile-setter, plumber, and electrician.

Can you just buy the design and act as your own general contractor? You won't need to with a bath dealer: He or she will provide a complete package, from design through installation. In this case, you'll probably pay a flat fee or a percentage of the total project that covers everything. If you choose an independent designer for the greater range of product choices, you'll pay an hourly rate or a flat fee for the design. The designer will place orders on products for you (especially important if you want to buy through a to-the-trade design center) to ensure that everything is acquired in the correct size and style. The bill may come to the designer or directly to you, depending on the arrangements made. You can then choose to take the implementation to a contractor or act as your own general contractor.

If you want to act as your own contractor, do some studying on what's involved. You'll need to be aware of local building codes and legal language to ensure that your contracts hold the subcontractors to working within the rules. You'll also need to

decision: See photos, get explanations, and talk to references.

Some bath designers have been qualified, through education, professional experience, and testing, as Certified Bath Designers, identifiable by the "CBD" designation after their names. (There is also an equivalent "CKD"–Certified Kitchen Designer–designation that may be earned, and many bath designers hold both.) A bath specialist who is a CBD is thoroughly versed in the "back-of-the-wall" aspects of design–electrical, plumbing, know how to apply for building permits and plan for inspections by building code officials as well as at least understand the basics of each function, so you'll know if a job is going seriously awry. Be patient, and keep in mind that building code enforcement is for your protection against unscrupulous or shoddy work.

Whomever you hire, you'll rely on their expertise to guide you through technical issues, and you'll count on their integrity in working within your budget. What's more, your experts and their crews will be in your home and around your family for the life of the project. So make sure they really deserve your trust!

CHECK THE BASICS

Check with the attorney general's office in your state and with your local Better Business Bureau to be sure there are no unresolved complaints against the professional you're considering. For contractors, ask to see property damage, liability, and workers' compensation insurance. (Don't just take their word for it. Tell them your lawyer insists you see each individual policy and note the policy number; dates the policy is in effect; and the name, address, and phone number of each company providing coverage. Before work starts, call to be sure policies are still in force.) If building permits are needed, make sure they're made out in the contractor's name, not yours.

Liking the professional you choose is important, because they'll be around your home and family for awhile. But before you sign on the dotted line, be sure to ask for photos of a number of bathroom designs they've executed, and ask them to explain the "before" situation—what client problems, both design and technical, they were required to solve. Also, be sure to ask for at least three or four references from clients for whom they've done bathrooms, specifically. Don't rely on how handsome the exterior of a house looks, how stunning a living room decor is, or how nice a new sunroom addition turned out. You want to see bathrooms and talk to their owners!

When you check references, ask if their projects were completed on schedule, if the pro was responsive to their calls, and if he or she kept them informed about the progress of the projects. If you'll be living in your home while the work is being done, ask if the workers left the place "broom clean" at night or in a mess, if they woke the baby with loud music, and if they were easy to live with. Ask if they'd hire the contractor again or recommend him or her to family and friends.

When you meet with your prospective professionals, be sure you have an elementary rapport with them. Do you believe they're knowledgeable? Honest? Pleasant and responsive? Reliable and unflappable? Do they seem interested in your needs, your lifestyle, and your dreams? If anything "just doesn't feel right," look further. Chemistry counts!

Finally, make sure the professional gives you a quote that fully describes the work, the specific products to be used (by brand name, type, model number, color, size, etc.), the costs, the starting and completion dates (plus conditions of, and penalties for, nonperformance), and the terms of payment. If it's a $1,500 job, you won't need a full-blown contract as you would for a job worth $15,000, but be sure the basics are covered in writing. It's your home and your money.

Surviving Your Bath Remodeling

I F YOU'RE REMODELING your only bath, the situation is much more challenging than if you're adding or expanding a second bath or simply redecorating or replacing fixtures. Losing your one bath, even for a few days, is tough, so if you're planning a second bath somewhere down the road, it may be worthwhile for you to switch projects and install the second bath before disabling the first (and only) one. Installers can sometimes work around the problem, keeping fixtures useable during at least part of the project, but a better alternative, depending on your situation, may be to rent a portable toilet booth like the kind used on construction sites and wash in the kitchen sink. Another option is to live somewhere else for the critical period of the project when fixtures are out of commission.

Obviously, you won't want to embark on remodeling your lone bathroom while trying to toilet train a toddler, but let's face it: Modern life is stressful. There's little point in waiting until "things" settle down to start your bath project, because that's unlikely to happen. Instead, use common sense to get the most out of your installation crew, save your house, and get your sanity back more quickly.

Before work begins, hold a preconstruction conference to give you and everyone involved in the project a chance to go over the details, ask questions, and give answers. Having a realistic understanding of what's involved with the project on a day-to-day basis will go a long way in helping you cope with the stress of disruption and inevitable mess. Work schedules should be reviewed at this time, and you should be given clear information on whom to contact, and how, if anything seems to be going wrong. Whoever is serving as your general contractor and hiring the subcontractor specialists should be responsible for orchestrating all the elements, including when workers and materials arrive. If either a scheduled crew or a scheduled delivery doesn't show up, contact the contractor. It does little good to rail at the workers who are there; the contractor should be reachable immediately by pager or cell phone, at least through his office. Here's where you'll be glad you asked prior clients how responsive this contractor was before you signed the contract!

As for delays, you can ask that the contract include a penalty clause that reduces your fee if the job is delayed for reasons that are not acts of God. However, the contractor may then want the contract to include a bonus if they bring the work in ahead of schedule. (Both of these clauses are common in commercial, but not residential, work.) Most contractors will try to give you an honest ballpark estimate of when they can start the work and when they expect to complete it, but problems on jobs that precede yours and problems they discover during your project can easily delay starting or finishing your project. Plan a solid cushion—say a month—for Murphy's Law to take effect, and don't schedule your job so that the work is supposed to be done two days before your daughter's at-home wedding.

Well before the crews arrive, brief your family thoroughly, and get answers to any questions they may have. Make sure the contractor has scheduled a dumpster and knows where it's to be installed on your property. When the dumpster arrives, finish

Designing a bath as beautiful as this one takes meticulous planning—from you and your contractor. Take the time to ask questions and go over every detail to ensure you end up with the bath you've always dreamed of.

any demising work you've agreed to do, and clean up the space. The day before, clear out the bathroom, and put drop cloths over furniture and floors in the hall and nearby rooms to protect them from dust, which can be considerable. Double-check with the contractor that, when the crews arrive, they'll be affixing sheets of clear plastic like curtains over doorways to contain the dust and debris and that they'll be removing the debris to the dumpster at the end of each day. (Your contract should specify that the work area will be left "broom clean" each night.) When the crews arrive, show them how and where to shut off and turn on the water. Then, stay out of the way except to answer questions and keep a general eye on things.

What if you want something different during the job? Changes can really add up, so don't handle them in an impromptu manner with a casual conversation. Be sure your contract includes a provision that "all changes will be handled through signed change orders," and look at what you're signing.

At the conclusion of the job, your contractor will accompany you through the project with a punch list to make sure every detail has been taken care of as agreed. Reputable professionals will be interested in making sure you're happy to sign off on the job and make that final payment. After all, they want you to provide that rave review for their next prospective customer!

Y OU'RE EAGER to start choosing your beautiful new fixtures, fittings, tiles, and more. But wait: Avoid the patchwork approach. You can stuff a poor clothing purchase into the back of your closet and throw a cover over the wrong sofa, but installed product is a lot harder to disguise. So, take a little time to learn about basic bathroom layouts, including plumbing and mechanical considerations that may affect your choices—and their costs. Then, reward yourself for your diligence by dipping into the basics of decorating success: how to use the toolbox of color, line, and shape to create a place that looks as good as it feels.

Timeless and pristine, white gives any style bath a classical sense of elegance and expansiveness. Generously scaled his-and-her sinks and an array of richly toned accents make this space even more inviting.

How your new bath will look is partly determined by the room's size and shape, but just as important is who will use it and what functions it will need to handle.

Master Bath

Located within the master bedroom (making it a suite) or adjacent to it, the master bath is usually the largest bath in the house. Designed for two, it may feature an extra-long vanity counter, a vanity with two sinks, or even two separate vanity sinks. In some baths, separate vanity sinks are located back-to-back in the center of the room or back-to-back on opposite walls, rather than side by side. Depending on the size of the room, you can use innovative floor plans to create a dramatic effect.

The master bath is where you may indulge in a separate soaking tub and shower, a whirlpool bath, a bidet, adjacent walk-in closets, an exercise area, a separate or semienclosed toilet compartment, full-length dressing mirrors, brass or gold-plated fittings, and other luxurious appointments. It's a spa built for two!

Family Bath

A bath shared by all family members is most often used by only one person at a time, except in the case of very young children. Usually, the family bath is located near the bedrooms; in a two-story house, there may be a full bath with a shower/tub upstairs and a powder room (sink and toilet only) or

Deep tones of wood, slate, and marble are set off by rich, golden-hued walls in this handsome master bath. A skylight helps offset the dark tones and makes the space dramatic.

a half bath (sink, toilet, and stall shower; no tub) on the first floor. Either way, the family bath gets a lot of use and wear. Surfaces need to be easy-to-clean and durable for kids' sake yet meet at least some of the adults' desire for an attractive space.

A good-size vanity helps, with a single sink (or better yet, a double sink for those rush times when several family members must wash up together) and plenty of storage cabinets above and below. Storage shared by kids and teens should be closed to keep clutter out of sight, and each family member should have at least one shelf of his or her own behind closed doors.

While a clear shower curtain or door will make the space look bigger, you may prefer an attractive opaque shower curtain for privacy. If space permits, you'll gain even more privacy with the toilet in its own compartment, ideally with a second entry door from the common hallway. If that's not feasible, locate the toilet away from the door, and screen it with a half-high partition.

Hang a towel ring or bar at the right level for each family member plus hooks for robes. As an antidote to the natural uproar, choose a soothing color scheme that will appeal to both sexes and will allow you to color-code towels for each family member without clashing. Add an attractive little alarm clock to this bath's accessories as a gentle reminder to share. These little touches not only make for a personality-filled bath, but they can also help keep the peace!

KIDS' BATH

When creating a bathroom for children and teenagers, you'll want to be especially attentive to issues of territory and safety. Here's where universal-access principles really come in handy, helping to create a space that will work well for users of all ages.

For starters, use a double vanity, if possible, or at least a large one. If space permits, install a separate stall shower and tub rather than the shower/tub combo, which is not as safe. And specify a shower-head that slides up and down on a pole; they're great for kids of any height and a boon to wheelchair users of any age.

To prevent squabbling, make sure each child has room for his or her own towels, robe, and personal care items, and color-code towels, storage bins, etc., to minimize mix-ups. If the bath is being shared by children of both sexes, choose a color scheme that appeals to both: blue and coral, for example, or green and yellow. Lighthearted tones in geometric stripes and plaids are fresh yet timeless.

Employ tile, scrubbable vinyl wallcovering, or enamel paint all the way up walls wherever possible. If children are of widely different ages, install a full-length (safety glass) mirror that all can use and towel hooks or bars at appropriate heights. Be sure to also put the light switch near the door low enough for younger users to reach.

Safety tips for kids' baths really apply to any bath. Insist on slip-resistant flooring, and make sure

This kids' bath's imaginative underwater theme goes swimmingly with a foolproof primary color scheme of red, yellow, and blue plus white. Rounded corners keep things safer, too. Wallcoverings: York Wallcoverings.

front corners on vanity countertops and cabinets are rounded. Ask for a slip-resistant tub floor if you must use a shower/tub combination. Use safety glass mirrors and safety glass on shower doors, and make sure all electrical outlets are grounded and located away from the sink or tub. It's a good idea to install grab bars (they require support behind the walls) to discourage youngsters from treating towel bars as grab bars.

Get an antiscald faucet that lets you preset water temperature limits (usually 120 degrees Fahrenheit) in a child's bath, and make sure the showerhead has a pressure-balancing valve that compensates for changes in water pressure and temperature. A sudden surge of hot water can do real damage with frightening speed, especially to children, who have thinner skin than adults do. It takes just three seconds of exposure to water at 140

degrees Fahrenheit for a young child to sustain a painful third-degree burn requiring a hospital visit!

Next to injury from burns and falling, poisoning and drowning are the most common hazards to children in the bath. For a few dollars, install safety latches on lower cabinets and on the toilet lid, and insist that teens be totally vigilant about keeping their personal care items stashed in upper cabinets.

POWDER ROOM/HALF BATH

The powder room (sink and toilet only) or the half bath (sink, toilet, and shower stall; no tub) is a versatile addition to any home. Tucked into the basement, it makes a family room or recreation room more comfortable. Next to the den or home office, a half bath becomes part of a guest suite. Near the dining room, it's convenient for dinner guests (but make sure the bath accesses from the hall, not directly from the dining room itself).

Often dubbed the "guest bath," this usually diminutive room can be decorated as creatively as you wish, depending on where it's located. Off the dining room, elegant touches include an ornate gilt mirror, high-end wallcovering or faux-finished wall treatments, gold or brass fittings, and embellished fingertip towels. In the basement, whimsical wall treatments and accessories can evoke a woodsy fishing cabin, breezy beach cabana, or other romanticized locale. Near the den, a half bath gains suite success when it's decorated in a similar style, whether garden-fresh or crisply tailored.

In any powder room or half bath, you'll probably want to save space with a good-looking pedestal sink and stash spare bathroom supplies in a separate, covered basket or box. You'll also want to expand space visually with large areas of mirror.

In ADDITION TO more baths, today's homes often sport more specialized baths than in the past. Easiest to create in newly constructed homes or additions, specialty baths can also be carved out of unused guest bedrooms, hallways, the space over the garage, or other existing areas. Here are a few of the most-wanted specialty baths.

MASTER SUITE

While many homes can accommodate a master bath adjacent to the master bedroom, a master suite has the bathroom actually incorporated into a section of the overall bedroom area, both enclosed behind a door that leads to the common hallway. Large or small, a master suite looks especially spacious and elegant when both the bedroom and the bathroom share a design scheme. Although the bedroom is largely soft furnishings and the bathroom is mostly hard-surface installed fixtures, you can incorporate the same motifs (neoclassical, English country, Early American, soft contemporary, etc.) in both, using the same color scheme.

You may elect to alter the proportions of each color to create variations on a theme. For example, an opulent European-inspired bedroom in wine with accents of hunter green, gold, and ivory may lead nicely into a master bath with hunter green fixtures, brass-gold fittings, and ivory ceramic tiles, sparked with towels and accessories in wine.

When designing the suite, you may want to avoid putting fixtures on the wall shared with the bedroom to minimize noise from a pressure-assist

In a spacious, glamorous bath, perhaps the most luxurious touch of all is the private toilet compartment. Glass block insets in the walls admit light from interior fixtures and the outdoors without compromising privacy.

toilet, shower, and so on. You can further buffer sound by putting bath cabinets and bedroom closets on opposite sides of a shared wall, with the bed on the far wall.

If possible, locate the bath on an outside wall to make a window possible, and make sure the walkway between the bedroom and the bath is easily accessible, wide enough, and free of obstructions, to be safe for users in the dark or when ill.

PRIVATE TOILET COMPARTMENT

With both halves of a couple rushing to get ready for work at the same time these days, a shared bathroom is under more demands. Even the closest pair often prefer a private toilet compartment, and bigger baths are beginning to reflect this desire.

Where your waste stack is (or can be) located will have a lot to do with where the toilet is located. If it's on a far wall and in a corner, a separate compartment is feasible. The compartment wall will run the full height of the room and should extend at least 3 feet in front of the toilet and a foot on each side; wider for universal accessibility. The compartment should be equipped with an easily accessible artificial light source plus a skylight or small window if at all possible. If there's no operable window, be sure to install an exhaust fan to keep the space fresh. You'll also want to make sure that there's enough space for a hanging cabinet above the toilet tank to house commonly needed supplies and that there's room for a small wastebasket on the floor. A pocket door makes privacy easier without sacrificing precious floor space.

If a totally private compartment isn't possible, look into designs that include a half-high partition that can be tiled the same as adjoining walls or a tall, hinged screen covered in fabric that coordinates with your room scheme. If the toilet is located in or near a corner, these solutions may be an acceptable compromise.

EXERCISE ROOM

You're going to jump into the shower right after you exercise anyway, right? So why not bring the exercise equipment to the bath area? That's the philosophy behind today's new exercise room baths. If your space is big enough, it may be right for you. Plan to put all bathroom fixtures on perimeter walls, and offset the door to allow space for one or two pieces of exercise equipment in the free area. Make sure you're not blocking the door or access to bathroom fixtures: Measure the space required for normal use of all equipment, and give them plenty of berth. Specify nonslip floor tiles to guard against slipping due to perspiration and bathing, and plan systems for ample ventilation, too.

LAUNDRY ROOM

While many laundry appliances have come out of the basement and up to the mud room or kitchen, others are being located near where dirty clothes first accumulate: the bedroom or bathroom. If you and your mate are alone in the house, you may want to put the laundry equipment in your master suite; if you share the house with children, you may prefer to house it in the kids' bathroom or a nearby guest bath.

Laundry appliances can tie into the same water supplies as the bathrooms, and preferred flooring—nonporous, nonslip tile—can be extended for both to create a neater look. If space is scanty, you may opt for a stacked washer/dryer unit, although these handle smaller loads than a typical family creates.

If you've got (or can find) the space, a combined bathroom/ exercise room is a very sensible luxury. This bright room combines health club amenities with home spa comforts. Windows: Andersen Windows, Inc.

Allow for plenty of overhead storage, preferably enclosed, for laundry supplies as well as hampers or other storage for sorting clothes. A pocket or folding door easily conceals the whole works from the rest of the bath, but you may want access on both ends of the laundry space so that laundry facilities can be used without going through the main bathroom area.

ADJACENT CLOSET

Closets between a bedroom and a bath make sense, and a dressing room area lined with roomy closets, all located next to a bath, is an even greater luxury you may want to consider. You might find part of the necessary space in a hallway closet, an unused area of the bedroom, or even a corner of the bath, provided they're contiguous. This is one place where telling your architect, contractor, or designer what you want can really pay off. They'll be on the lookout for ways to shoehorn extra closets into

even a tiny space for you. Once the basic space is in, consult a professional closet design firm, or explore the closet fittings section of your local home store for ways to maximize the closet space you have. You'll surely find ideas that work in the rest of your closets, too!

HOW BIG IS BIG ENOUGH?

The typical 5×7-foot bath "footprint" makes a generously sized powder room and a decent-size half bath. It can be sufficient for a kids' bath if no more than two will be using it at once and if you've cleverly planned in separate storage for each child. It may even be enough for a master bath if what you most want is just the convenience of the plumbing in or near the master bedroom. A 5×7-foot space won't be enough, however, for a lavish master bath with extra fixtures (bidet, separate whirlpool tub, sauna, etc.), and it may also be a bit skimpy for a shared family bath by today's standards.

You can make up the difference visually by keeping the design scheme calm, using mirrors liberally, and specifying cabinetry that makes the best use of space (consider lazy Susans; cubbyholes; and small drawers, such as lingerie or spice drawers). But to really add space, you'll need to see if you can steal a few feet from an adjacent closet or unused area of a neighboring room or hallway, or even bump out a mini-addition. In most rooms, another 18 inches wouldn't mean much, but they can make a surprising difference in the bath!

UPSTAIRS, DOWNSTAIRS: WHERE TO PUT THE BATH?

It's a bigger challenge to install a new bath in an existing home than to remodel a bath or to build a bath into a new house. That's because "back-of-the-wall" plumbing and mechanical requirements have to be installed within an existing wall, and you won't know what that involves until the wall is opened. It's an even bigger challenge when you're installing the bath on an upper floor or in the basement. While a professional can make it work, you'll want to be aware of the issues.

A basement bath requires special planning for below-grade plumbing. A space 16 square feet (30×75 inches) is adequate for a toilet and a sink; to include a shower or a tub, you'll need a space about 35 square feet (5×7 feet, which is the size of a standard bathroom). Building codes allow ceiling heights of 84 inches for basement baths, which is 6 inches lower than for other living areas. This variance will come in handy if your ceiling height is restricted by pipes or ductwork.

The most critical factor in installing a basement bathroom is locating drains and vent stacks. Get-

ting hot and cold water to the space is a matter of splicing into existing supply lines, but pumping wastewater out may be more difficult. All bathroom fixtures must drain into the main drain line, which is a 3- to 4-inch diameter pipe that enters the basement through the floor above and exits the basement through a wall or the floor. Accessing the main drain for a new basement toilet may mean cutting through a concrete floor—a difficult task. Also, new fixtures can only be located a limited distance from the existing drain line, and extensions to the line must slope down at the rate of at least $1/4$ inch per foot.

If tying into existing lines below floor level is not practical, you'll need a sewage ejector—an electric pump attached to a holding tank that pumps sewage up through a discharge pipe into the main house drain. Sewage ejectors are fairly costly but not much more noisy than today's pressure-assist toilets. You'll also need to tie new drains to existing vent stacks or install a new stack, most often alongside the exterior of your house in an inconspicuous location.

A new upstairs bath must also tie into the existing main drain line and vent stack, but this is usually an easier accomplishment because upper floors and walls are not made of concrete. Not to mention, in upper floors, gravity works with, not against you in moving waste downward.

Regardless of where you plan to locate your new bath, you know installing it isn't for amateurs. Unless plumbing and mechanical engineering are your lines of work, consult the experts, and save your energy for choosing fixtures and decorative treatments!

IF YOU'VE EVER WONDERED why many bathrooms are back-to-back or why professionals tell you to avoid moving fixtures, it's because of all the plumbing and mechanical systems you can't see. "Back-of-the-wall" systems include various pipes to bring fresh water into the room, pipes to bring hot water from your hot-water heater, pipes to carry away wastewater, more pipes to carry away waste, vent stacks to keep pressure equalized and to prevent sewer gasses from entering the house, and on and on. Even if your bath is on the third floor of your house, its systems have to route up to the roof and down to the systems buried in your lawn on the ground level. Bottom line: The fixtures are just the end point of an entire system.

If you really want to know about all this in detail, the information is available. If not, simply respect that the system is complex, and be aware that your installers not only need to solve whatever problems they encounter in your individual house, but they also need to solve it within the confines of rigorous building codes designed to safeguard your family's health and your home's safe function. Your understanding can help you get the best job possible from your installers.

If you're remodeling an existing bath, you'll have to decide whether you want to incur the expense of moving basic fixtures and changing the basic layout. If you're only moving a fixture a few feet for a slightly better look, you may elect to go ahead—or not, given the cost. If the existing bath layout really bothers you or is unworkable, your top priority may be to relocate fixtures. What's important is that you understand that this is much more complex than, say, moving a king-size bed from one wall of your bedroom to another!

Virtually every bathroom uses one of the following three basic layouts:

- **One-wall layout.** One-wall baths have the toilet, sink, and combination shower/tub plumbing aligned along one wall, making for a relatively long, narrow bathroom. One-wall layouts are often used where the simplest solution is to cut off the "end" of a long room and dedicate it to bath fixtures. This layout is also frequently used for powder room or half bath layouts. You may find extra fixtures, such as a bidet, a separate tub, and a separate shower in a one-wall bath, but it's not common.

A rather exotic but uncluttered bath is achieved with the simplicity of a one-wall layout. Plumbing for the two vanity sinks, the toilet, and the tub all lie along the same wall.

- **Two-wall layout.** Two-wall baths usually have the toilet and sink on one wall and the shower/tub combo (or separate shower and tub) on the other. You might also find the toilet and bidet on one wall and the shower/tub and the sink on the other, depending on the length of each wall. A two-wall layout offers a desirable sense of enclosure, but care must be taken to ensure that fixtures are placed far enough from each other and from the door for safety and comfortable use.

- **Three-wall layout.** A three-wall layout, with the toilet on one wall, sink on another, and combination shower/tub on the third, is a space-conserving solution that can put every fixture within a step of the others. It's also the layout you're likely to see in a master bath with numerous extra fixtures such as a bidet, more than one sink, and a separate tub and shower. If you are remodeling an old bath and want to install a number of new upgrades, a room that's already plumbed in the three-wall layout may be the easiest to work with.

Above Left: *This confidently styled bath has a two-wall layout that features a bidet and toilet on one wall and a tub and sink on an adjacent wall.* Manufacturer: Briggs Plumbing Products, Inc. **Left:** *This expansive bath features a three-wall layout with the toilet (in its own private compartment) and double sinks on one wall, the shower on another, and the tub on the third.*

Y OUR FOCUS may be on basic bath fixtures and surfacing materials, but your comfort in the room will be affected by the often-overlooked fixtures that provide light and ventilation. You may also want supplementary heating in the bath, most often electrical. These fixtures will require adequate electrical wiring, which may involve pulling wire through existing plaster walls and ceilings. Plan for more electrical access than you think you'll need, since your needs are likely to increase over time as new technology becomes available.

VENTILATING FANS

If you think a ventilating fan in your new bath is a nice-to, not a need-to, think again. An open window isn't feasible all year-round in most climates, and it's just not as efficient as a ventilating fan at replacing odor-carrying, stale air with fresh air. What's more, an open window is even less efficient at reducing the harmful humidity in a bath. All those showers and baths take their toll not just on your new wallcovering but also on your home's basic structure, as hidden moisture builds up in today's well-insulated houses. A good ventilating fan is a relatively small investment that will make any bath—especially a shared one—more comfortable and will help preserve your home's infrastructure. Models that include lights and infrared heating panels as well as fans are especially practical.

LIGHTING

In the bathroom, as in the kitchen, adequate lighting isn't just aesthetic, it's a real safety issue. So don't skimp here. You'll need general lighting to find your way around the room; task lighting for shaving, hairstyling, and fixing that splinter; and,

Mirrored walls maximize the already ample light from this spacious bath's recessed lighting fixtures and skylight in the ceiling.

in some baths, mood lighting. One dramatic and popular solution, theatrical mirror lighting, can handle more than one job, and lighter-colored walls and surfaces will maximize the effect of available light.

COMFORT AND SAFETY

Your installer has a legal obligation to comply with building codes, which keep changing to reflect new understanding about hazards in the built environment—in this case, your bathroom. But there is a host of other proven guidelines your installer

Grab bars, an adjustable showerhead, and plenty of clear floor space for a wheelchair are just a few of the features that make this bath accessible for any user.

should be employing to make your new bath safe and comfortable.

The National Kitchen & Bath Association (NKBA) has developed a punch list of 41 guidelines that range from the essential to the highly recommended. Here are just a few:

- clear space at doorways of at least 32 inches wide
- at least 48 inches of clear space in front of a toilet and 16 inches on each side (measured from the fixture's centerline)
- clear space of at least 15 inches on each side of a sink to the wall (measured from the sink's centerline)
- shower doors that open into the bathroom so you can get out
- safety rails next to tubs (and definitely no steps!)
- tub faucets reachable from outside as well as inside the tub
- compartment toilet space of at least 36×66 inches
- grab bars able to hold 300 pounds

A number of the NKBA guidelines foster "universal access." Important developments in bath design have come from the federal Americans with Disabilities Act (ADA), which has transformed public and commercial buildings from off-limits to accessible. Universal access has come to mean not just access for people with traditional "handicaps" but increased livability for children, senior citizens, pregnant women, and others who have had to make do with uncomfortable or dangerous fixtures. Grab bars and wider doorways are just two universal access benefits that can make your bath more comfortable today—and through all your tomorrows.

ONCE YOU'VE MADE SURE your new bath will meet your physical needs, you can go on to the fun part: making decorating decisions.

Self-expression is important, but the most satisfying room solutions don't throw design principles to the wind. The sense that some approaches "just feel right" and that others don't is at least partly inborn in humans. Luckily, there are a few basic design principles you can use to satisfy the innate sense of "what works." With practice, you can express yourself and still play by the rules, confident that you won't stray too far from what appeals to the human eye and psyche.

A modest room that uses design principles cleverly will beat a much more expensive one that doesn't, hands-down. So, whether your bath is a superspa or a tiny powder room, make sure these principles are at work.

THE VIRTUE OF BALANCE

Balance is the sense that objects in a space (or fixtures and furniture in a room) are weighted equally on both sides of a given center point. You know when you see a fireplace mantel with a huge vase on one end and a tiny candlestick on the other that the balance is off. It makes you innately uncomfortable. Keep the following tips in mind to achieve the right balance in your bath.

- **Symmetrical balance.** To achieve equilibrium, a big vase near each end of your mantel or, even better, a big vase in the middle with a smaller candlestick on each end, would provide symmetrical balance. You know something has symmetrical balance if you could draw an imaginary line down the middle of the view and each half would exactly mirror the other. An example of symmetrical balance in the bathroom would include a vanity with a mirror centered on the wall above and matching sconces flanking the mirror on each side.

  Traditional, classical European design and architecture, in which symmetrical design was born, rely heavily on this type of design for their dignity and reposeful qualities. As an offshoot of European models, early American country styles are also at home with symmetrical balance, although the materials used will be more casual.

- **Asymmetrical balance.** More difficult to achieve but, for that reason, more sophisticated, asymmetrical balance relies on creating a sense of equal mass on both sides of an imaginary center point. In our mantel example, a big vase on one end could be balanced by five small candlesticks that, placed close together, create a mass equal to the vase. In the bathroom, asymmetrical balance might be achieved by a hefty tub on one wall balanced by a toilet and matching bidet taking up the same length on the opposite wall.

  Asymmetrical balance is usually associated with an Asian or modern design aesthetic and works well when the ambience is adventurous, as the effect is a more dynamic balance. At its most confident, asymmetrical balance may poise an object against a blank space or, in architect-speak, a "void" of the same visual weight.

  Of course, color, shine, texture, and other elements affect visual balance as well. A white vase will require fewer, lighter-colored candlesticks to balance it than will a scarlet red or eggplant purple one. Your best bet is to study rooms that appeal to

ronment. Too much repetition is boring or irritating; too little is unnerving, resulting in a sense of chaos. The human brain instinctively seeks out repetitive patterns in its effort to make sense of an environment and, when it finds these patterns, experiences a sense of pleasure. You can tap into this hard-wired need and give even a small room big appeal.

To achieve this rhythm, repeat a sequence of color, shape, line, or motif, interspersed with "rests" of contrasting colors and shapes that will help the eye pick out the pattern. For example, black/white, repeated over and over, is a simple rhythm; a more complex pattern might be green-green/blue-blue/ivory-ivory/crimson, repeated. (This rhythm, with a smaller dose of crimson, also illustrates a tried-and-true design concept that advancing, bright colors like red are often best used in a smaller proportion than cool or neutral colors.)

In a bathroom, the shine of smooth ceramic may be interspersed with the matte richness of limestone or the fluffiness of cotton towels. If the ceramic and limestone are both tones of white and the towels

While the objects on each side of this doorway aren't the same, the visual mass, or volume, on each side is. The effect is a pleasing asymmetrical balance. Fixtures: Sottini.

you, especially professionally designed ones. You'll begin to see why one room "works" visually and another doesn't. When in doubt, consult a design professional for your bath. With so much installed product that can't be rearranged, you'll want to get it right the first time.

YOU'VE GOT RHYTHM

Rhythm is the quality of pleasing repetition in a piece of music, an artwork or artifact, or an envi-

and ceramic accent pieces are in a range of pinks and reds, you have two rhythms going: one of texture and one of color, which adds further interest. Again, your eye will tell you *what* works; your knowledge will tell you *why* it works.

Make Your Point With Emphasis

Emphasis is the creation of a focal point, a dominant item of interest in an environment. The eye is initially drawn to this focal point and returns there for a rest.

Designers usually counsel clients to find or create a focal point in each room as a first step toward organizing the space attractively. There is a hierarchy of focal points: A large bay window beats a fireplace, a fireplace beats a TV in a wall unit, a TV in a wall unit beats an impressive armoire, and so on. But generally, the most eye-catching, large item in a room will be the focal point. In the bedroom, it's usually the bed; in the bathroom, it may be an imposing double vanity with a pair of mirrors or a big soaking tub angled in the corner opposite the door.

You can give the natural focal point in a room even more emphasis or build up the importance of another area to create an alternative focal point by using elements that naturally catch the eye. Colors brighter than those in the rest of the space; mirrors; lighting sources; or an object that contains movement, such as an aquarium or a large set of wind chimes, are all natural focal points. Eye-catching attributes on secondary pieces also help you create balance in the room so one wall doesn't appear too heavy.

Just don't overdo secondary areas: Make sure a viewer can instantly perceive the focal point.

When a room setting is appealing (restful yet interesting), it's usually because all three principles—balance, rhythm, and emphasis—are working together. Once you experience the satisfaction of using these principles in the small space of your bath, you may be inspired to go on and retool the bigger rooms in your house!

Although this bath boasts a number of impressive elements, this unusual, cone-shape sink and coordinating round mirror serve as the focal point by virtue of their positioning opposite the entry door.

EVERYTHING in your bathroom includes design elements that can be used to achieve balance, rhythm, and emphasis. These elements occur naturally together, so it may take a bit of practice to see them. Once you do, you'll be able to make the often small corrections that give your bath maximum eye appeal.

COLOR

Color is the most compelling element. Whole books have been written on how to use color, but a few basic techniques are worth noting here.

Light colors reflect light and make a space or an object look larger and airier; dark colors absorb light and make them look smaller and denser.

Contrasting colors stop the eye, breaking up space and making it look smaller. The same or similar colors across surfaces allow the eye to keep moving and unify a space, making the whole area look larger.

Warm colors, such as red, orange, or yellow, reflect light and advance toward the viewer, making the item or wall seem closer and larger. The same goes for pastel versions of these tones—pink, coral, peach, and cream—but the effect is modified by how much white is in the mix. Pale pink won't come at you the way hot pink will, but it still imparts a sense of warmth.

Cool colors like blue, green, and violet absorb light and recede from the viewer, making the item or wall seem farther away and smaller.

To maximize a sense of spaciousness and repose in the bath, you might opt for a scheme of light colors accented by cool colors in pastel strengths to keep the contrasts low. However, many people pre-

A pure white bath looks clean, airy, and spacious because white or very pale colors reflect light, visually expanding the room. It's especially useful for small-space baths. Designer: Dieter Sieger, Sieger Design. Fixtures: Dornbracht USA.

When you want to draw attention to special features or just create a sense of visual excitement in a room, call on bright, advancing colors to do the job. Designer: Dieter Sieger, Sieger Design. Fixtures: Dornbracht USA.

Dark blue items visually recede, yellow ones advance; used together, they create a lively scheme that breaks up the monotony of an all-white setting. Designer: Dieter Sieger, Sieger Design. Fixtures: Dornbracht USA.

fer pastel tones of warmer colors—blush tones, for example—for their complexion-enhancing qualities. And some prefer to go with, rather than against, a bath's small dimensions by using dark, rich colors for maximum coziness. The choice is yours!

If your bathroom includes a window, keep in mind the room's exposure to the sun. Light from the north and the east is cool, with light rays coming from the blue end of the spectrum. South and west light is warm because the sun's rays come from the red end.

Artificial lighting also affects how colors look. Except for special "full spectrum" lightbulbs that mimic natural light, you can expect that fluorescent light will give a cool blue-green tint, while incandescent light provides a warm yellow-red glow. Whatever the light in your bath, you can cozy up a chilly space with cheerful jonquil yellow paint or tame a high-temperature spot with iced lilac or aqua. Try it!

COLOR SCHEMING

To understand color relationships, imagine a color wheel with colors appearing in this order: red, red-orange, orange, yellow-orange, yellow, yellow-green, green, blue-green, blue, blue-violet, violet, red-violet, and back to red. This is the order in which colors appear in a rainbow. Tints of colors are made by adding white (e.g., red-orange plus white gives us coral). Shades of colors are made by adding black (e.g., blue-green plus black creates teal). This information comes in handy when you're trying to create a scheme of colors that look well together.

Start with a color you love, and plan your room using one of the following proven schemes:

- **Monochromatic.** This color scheme uses one color, repeated throughout the room in various shades and tints. Many of today's high-end baths use this sophisticated approach with luxurious natural materials and complex, neutral colors ranging from ivory to tan—a look suitable to either a classical traditional space or a very contemporary one. For a Victorian charmer, a monochromatic scheme might be based on a run of red, from pale cameo pink through rose and deep wine. Monochromatic schemes depend heavily on varying textures and other elements to add interest.

- **Analogous.** The easiest schemes to create, analogous schemes use a range of colors that are side by side on the color wheel plus shades and tints of those colors. For example, blue-violet, blue, and blue-green, in tones that range from icy periwinkle to deep teal, make an underwater fantasy bath. Yellow-orange, yellow, and yellow-green, in tones from cantaloupe to honeydew melon, make a cheery and refreshing spot.

- **Complementary.** Innately interesting, complementary schemes are based on a pair of colors that lie opposite each other on the color wheel plus tints and shades of these colors. The most appealing schemes tend to use one color in a much lighter version than the other. For example, where a fire engine red and kelly green scheme would be jarring, pale pink plus evergreen is lovely, and a blue-orange color scheme beguiles in royal blue plus peach. The complementary scheme of yellow and violet can be regal in gold and purple or springtime-pretty in jonquil and iris tones.

- **Split complementary.** This attractive scheme uses the colors on each side of its opposite. For example, blue-green (perhaps as aqua or teal) plus orange (peach) and red (pink) for tropical flair or yellow plus red-violet (orchid) and blue-violet (periwinkle) for a spring garden look.

- **Double-split complementary.** Often seen in designer fabrics (which you can always copy, including the proportions of each color), this sophisticated scheme uses two colors on each side of a color plus the two colors on each side of its complement. For example, if you like red and true blue, shake it up with red-orange and red-violet plus blue-green and blue-violet. Notice we're still using only four colors.
- **Triad.** This scheme uses three colors equidistant from each other on the color wheel. For example, red, blue, and yellow make a cheery kid's room or, toned down to wine, navy, and old ivory, an elegant Federal room.

All of these schemes can be cut with lots of white for a refreshing look or accents of gray or black for drama. Most can also accept neutral tan, brown, and taupe accents, and the green of living plants. Play with color chips to see what looks best to you. Then, pick one color to be the dominant one (usually the lightest color), and use it most liberally. Choose another color to be the secondary color (often a midtone) and one or two other colors as tertiary, accent colors (usually the brightest or darkest tones).

Try to corral bath clutter in all its many colors. Some people even decant shampoos into containers that coordinate with their bathrooms to

Right: *Tumbled marble and terra-cotta tiles add rich texture to this elegantly rustic bath. Spiral-embellished accent tiles create not only another layer of opulent texture, they add the flourish of a classical pattern.*

keep down the "visual chatter." Try it, and you'll find the whole space more visually relaxing.

TEXTURE AND PATTERN

Everything in your bath has a visible texture as well as a color, so it pays to be aware of it. Because a bath needs to be water-resistant and easy-to-clean, almost all surfaces are hard and smooth: glazed ceramic wall tile, marble or laminate vanity tops, porcelain fixtures, metal fittings, glass, and mirror. To provide a pleasing contrast, consider unglazed or matte-finish tiles for floors (safer, too!) and tumbled marble for walls. Easy ways to add texture to any bath are fluffy towels and cozy rugs secured to the floor with rug pads or nonslip tape.

Texture and its cousin, pattern, may appear together or separately. A vanity cabinet of oak, with its coarse, pronounced grain, introduces more texture and pattern than smooth-grained maple; faux-finished or antiqued cabinets have the same physical texture as those painted a solid color but offer more pattern. Both texture and pattern affect the visual "busy-ness" of a room, and more makes the space look smaller.

LINE AND SHAPE

Line and shape occur in the bath as design elements that affect how the room appears. For example, the vertical lines of wall cabinets, windows, the shower stall, and doors can make a room look taller; horizontal lines in the edges of the vanity and tub can make it look broader. Floor tiles contribute to line as well: Tiles laid diagonally make the floor appear larger than those laid parallel to the walls.

The traditional 5×7 bath with an 8- to 10-foot ceiling is taller than it is broad, so creating an illusion of height is seldom necessary. If you're fortunate enough to have a larger bath, use the same techniques you would for a bedroom or other room to keep height in balance with other dimensions.

Shape is less of a problem in baths than in other rooms. Elsewhere, you'd have to make sure to include a round table or oval-backed chairs to relieve the too-rectangular aspect of windows, doors, and storage furniture. But fortunately for visual appeal (and safety), most bath fixtures have rounded sides that contrast nicely to the squared-off shape of the room. Obviously, the more drawers, divided-light windows, towels, and tiles in the room, the more rectangular and square elements there are. Balance these with cathedral-topped cabinet doors, Palladian windows, round drawer pulls, and other curvy elements.

SPACE AND FORM

Space and form are the architect's tools for creating balance in the largest sense of the word. Space, or voids, have a real presence; they are not just the absence of form and are especially important when creating asymmetrical balance. In the bath, you'll immediately sense when space and form are out of whack (e.g., when all fixtures are on one wall with no balancing cabinetry or area of interest on the opposite wall).

Form includes mass as well as shape that you can modify with visual techniques. For instance, a small bath with a conventional shower/tub combo looks even more cramped with a busily patterned,

dark-colored shower curtain, no matter how pretty, taking up most of one wall. Replace it with a clear liner or a glass door, and the mass recedes to the far shower wall. By the same token, white cabinets look less massive than cabinets of the same dimension in natural oak.

Most people feel more comfortable when the largest eye-level masses in a room are not blocking their line of sight into the room. A shower stall or tub set behind the door or on the opposite wall will make a bath look larger than that same form set close to the entryway. A sink, even one in a vanity, is below eye level, so it may work nicely along the right side of a room near the door. Toilets are an exception, although their profile is low. If you'd like the toilet out of sight, screen or enclose it with a full- or half-height partition out of the line of sight of the entryway. It's the mass of the partition, not the toilet, that then determines its placement in the room.

Suppose your budget won't allow moving fixtures to the most visually appropriate walls. Use the visual techniques of color and line to make a mass appear less or more prominent and to achieve balance. As long as you make sure they reflect something attractive, you can use mirrors abundantly in the bath to fool the eye, bring in more light, create a sense of depth, draw attention to a focal point on the opposite wall, and more. Even a modest effort will yield big results!

With a designer to help make good use of this oddly shaped space, these homeowners got the separate shower and tub they craved; a large sink; ample storage; and a stylish, sleek look overall. (The sink is also universally accessible—a nice bonus.) Designer: Ann M. Morris, CKD, CBD, Ann Morris Interiors, Ltd. Fixtures: Kohler; fittings: Grohe; floor and wall tiles: Waterworks.

Components of Design

SHOPPING FOR TILE, fixtures, and other products for your

new bathroom can be great fun—if you know what

you're looking for and how it will meet your needs.

Today's bath remodeling scene is so full of fabulous

innovations and glamorous attractions, you're likely to

be distracted if you don't shop with a plan. So check out

your options in terms of function and budget first. Then

you can indulge in the fun of choosing among items you

know you'll still feel good about years from now!

Sculptural in form but obviously functional, this custom tub and double shower make a dramatic modern design statement that's one of a kind.

Fixtures: The Big Basics

BATHROOM FIXTURES and their fittings have changed in style over the years since indoor plumbing first transformed human existence, but their functions have undergone only minor changes. You may opt to replace a damaged or worn fixture and keep the rest, or you may replace the entire suite. In fact, replacing fixtures without relocating them is one of the most popular, cost-effective ways to redo a bath.

PEDESTAL AND WALL-HUNG SINKS

For a diminutive powder room or an elegant, lightly scaled look in any bath, pedestal and wall-hung sinks are just the ticket. Enameled cast iron (not steel, which chips easily), vitreous china, stainless steel, solid surfacing, and even colorful art glass (specially tempered, of course) are all used for free-standing sinks. Versatile styles range from nostalgi-

Grand gesture, tiny space: A dazzling powder room's focal point is this spectacular one-of-a-kind sink bowl on its own custom-made copper stand. Designer: Lori W. Carroll, ASID. Manufacturer: Alchemy Glass & Light.

cally traditional to space-age modern; at the very high end, pedestal sinks are made of semiprecious stones, such as agate or rose quartz, or with opulent hand-painted basins featuring lavish illustrations.

A bonus: Pedestal and wall-hung sinks are easily accessible to wheelchair users, and the wall-hung models can be set at just the right height. Sinks may be skirted to provide for hidden storage; glass or wood shelves can be installed above for open storage.

LAVATORY (IN-COUNTER) SINKS

If you need the countertop and extra storage space a vanity can provide, a sink, usually of vitreous china, can be dropped in. Undermount models attach to the underside of the counter; self-rimming sinks with rolled, finished edges rest on top of the counter. (A 1950s-era sink with a stainless-steel rim is less prevalent and harder to keep clean.) Undermount and self-rimming models may be mounted onto virtually any type of counter: ceramic tile, marble, or even marine-finished wood. The latest look in self-rimming sinks is a simple bowl in hammered metal, art glass, water-resistant wood, or

Traditional or contemporary, pedestal sinks are a classic solution for small-space baths. Sleek modern lines give this pedestal sink a timeless, sculptural air. Wallcovering: Seabrook Wallcoverings, Inc.

other attractive material that rests entirely above the countertop. A popular, often economical choice is an integral bowl seamlessly fused to the counter-top. This type of sink is usually made of marble composite (cultured marble), solid surfacing, or other synthetic material. Vanity sinks may be any geometric shape, including round and hexagonal; corner sinks are also available. Porcelain fixtures are offered with hand-painted traditional or modern motifs that make them literal works of art.

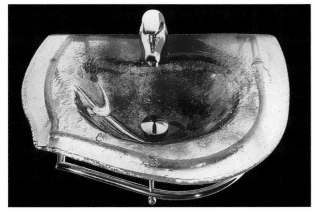

"Glass-fusion" sinks combine metal oxides with glass for a look that is both flowingly organic and strikingly contemporary. Like handmade art glass, each piece is unique. Sink: AquaDreams Ltd.

With all of today's fabulous fashion colors and designs, making a choice is a challenge. Dark colored lavs are dramatic and don't show grime as much as pastel or white lavatories do, but they are easily marked with soap scum and hard-water mineral deposits. Exotic colors may be enchanting or off-putting to a prospective buyer, especially in the hard-to-remove tub. If you're planning to stay in your home for a long time, you can indulge your personal preferences, but if there's a chance you'll be moving in a few years, think twice. Remember: Classic white, bone, and gray fixtures can be set off by virtually any color in towels, rugs, window treatments, wallcoverings, and accessories.

Fixtures are available in a variety of materials. Vitreous china is a classically beautiful choice for all fixtures. Porcelainized cast iron is an option for sinks, shower stalls, and tubs, but it's very heavy, difficult to maneuver into an upstairs bathroom, and just about impossible to remove except with a sledgehammer. Enameled or porcelainized steel chips and dents more easily than cast iron and doesn't hold heat as well, but it's less expensive and relatively lightweight. For integral sinks and counters, cultured marble made of marble dust in a cast polymer is popular and economical. Solid-surfacing material made of polyester or acrylic solids is costlier than cultured marble but more long-lasting. Acrylic and fiberglass may be used separately or together; formulations of either may appear as a backing or a surface material.

A translucent pedestal sink and a frosty space divider with a mirrored vanity shelf create a coolly modern design solution. Manufacturer: American Standard.

Classical tile surrounds this tub for a timelessly opulent look.
Designer: Emmye Otto, CKD, Rutt of Atlanta.

coordinate the fixtures' overall color and decorating style for a cohesive look. You can even visit an architectural salvage outlet and scout out pieces, modern as well as vintage, that make your decorating statement. One caution: Buy your fixtures and fittings at the same time to be sure they'll fit each other. You don't want to fall in love with a sink that needs a centerspread faucet after you've bought a widespread model!

BATHTUBS

Most conventional bathtubs are recessed—designed to fit into a recess in the bath with three sides hidden by walls and the fourth side an open, finished front. Recessed tubs are 30 to 33 inches wide and can be anywhere from 42 to 72 inches long, but most are 60 inches. Most recessed bathtubs have the space-saving combination tub/shower, but this style is not the safest. The smooth, sloping sides of tubs are kind to backsides but treacherous under wet feet, and experts much prefer a separate tub and shower. A short, soaking tub and an angled, corner shower may make this possible even in a skimpy bath.

Other bathtub models include the corner tub, a space-efficient way to provide for a whirlpool; a freestanding tub such as the vintage claw-foot style used to create a nostalgic look; and the platform tub with the exposed side covered in tile or other floor-matching material to give a "sunken-tub" effect. This last style is at home both in a very modern bath and in a classical bath inspired by ancient Rome.

WHIRLPOOL TUBS

More than any other fixture, the whirlpool tub symbolizes the luxurious new style of baths since the

New synthetics and combinations appear regularly on the marketplace, but china remains the timeless choice at all price points and makes it possible to completely coordinate all of your fixtures. However, if you are having a special tub or shower constructed rather than using a prefabricated unit, you may have other fixtures made from different materials. While toilets are almost always vitreous china, a sink can be made of wood (finished in tough plastic), stainless steel (look for 18-gauge not 20), or even ceramic tile. These choices let you late 1980s. Many whirlpool tubs are 4×5 feet, and some are much larger, but if you need to keep your existing bath footprint, scout out one that's 5 feet long but as narrow as a standard-size bathtub. If you can change the footprint but not the overall square footage of your bath, look for a whirlpool tub/shower combo or, better yet, a corner whirlpool and an angled shower.

Whirlpool tubs are usually either top-of-the-line cast iron or somewhat less costly acrylic and composites. They are most often recessed or, especially if they're large, built into platforms. Many of the early designs featured steps up to the tub without a handrail. Nowadays, this extremely dangerous design is avoided in favor of steps with a decorative, secure handrail or a higher, wide platform that allows bathers to sit on the edge of the whirlpool and swing their legs in. Also for safety's sake, make sure your design lets you reach the controls from outside the tub.

Another safety issue your installer will need to address is the weight problem (not yours—the whirlpool's!). Many homes' structures can't take the huge added weight of a whirlpool tub, the large volume of water, and the people using it, especially on the second floor, so additional shoring up will be necessary. Don't skip this step: You don't want to end up in the living room in your birthday suit!

A whirlpool tub with a waterfall feature is the centerpiece of this handsomely appointed traditional bath. Recessed wood paneling in 18th-century style integrates the bath into the room. **Whirlpool tub: Kohler.**

Seaworthy teak walls make an unusual, handsome shower stall that provides the option of a handheld shower or a steam shower. Designer: Lynn Monson, ASID, CKD, CBD, CID, Monson Interior Design, Inc. Steam unit: Steamist; handheld shower: Hansgrohe.

Whirlpool amenities include an in-line heater to maintain warmth without "topping off" the water, two-speed motors, touch-pad controls, and more. A handheld shower extension in the whirlpool tub is an option but requires awkward, one-handed hair washing, so most people add a separate shower.

SHOWERS

At the very least, you'll need a 36×36-inch space for a stall shower. It may be built in with only the slightest slope of the floor toward the drain, eliminating the need for a shower door, or you may opt for swing-out doors. With controls set into the wall, even a conventional tub/shower can offer the latest showering amenities. Modular shower systems are available that let you customize them with a choice of different shower floors, walls, and fittings. For example, multiple showerheads are great, and if you can install them into opposite walls, even an ordinary 60-inch tub can be a shower for two. A handheld showerhead with a wall-mounted pole that offers various height stations is great for kids or the disabled.

TOILETS

Typically made of vitreous china, toilets are available in several basic styles. The old-fashioned two-piece style with a round bowl mounted to the floor and a tank very high on the wall is available from a few manufacturers for nostalgic settings. The more familiar, traditional "close-coupled" model has a separate water tank mounted on a round bowl. The contemporary one-piece model, or "low boy," features a tank and bowl in one piece. If you've got the room, a sophisticated alternative is an elongated bowl, about two inches longer than the standard model in front. It's available in either

For hydrotherapy value, give a tub a "dry run" before buying it to be sure water jets are positioned comfortably for you. Look for jets that let you adjust the proportion of air and water (more air means a more vigorous massage) and the stream's direction.

Think twice about a giant tub for two: You may prefer to spend the money and floor space on other amenities unless you're among those rare couples who actually have the time to enjoy the tub together.

A "sunflower" shower-head is a vintage style that's new again. While your shower might not be outdoors with stone walls and have a teak chair as a seat, this setting is proof that you have lots of creative choices.

two-piece or one-piece designs. For tall or older people, models with bowls 18 inches from the floor are more comfortable than the standard 14½ to 15 inches. These usually come in two-piece units.

You may also choose between "gravity-assist" and "pressure-assist" models in any style. Toilets produced since January 1, 1994, are mandated by U.S. law to use no more than 1.6 gallons of water per flush. (Older models use 3.5 to 10 gallons per flush.) Opinions on this mandate vary. Reducing the amount of water used conserves water and eases the burden on sewage-treatment plants, but consumers find that some models, including many of the low-priced and midpriced models that rely solely on gravity assistance, don't do the job with one flush. To aid flushing, the new gravity-assist models of the two-piece variety are taller and slimmer than in the past and have steeper bowls.

Some homeowners have gone to the length of buying "bootleg" 3.5-gallon toilets in Canada, and some plumbing professionals have even expressed concern about potential public health dangers caused by inadequate flushing. While the jury is still out, other consumers have elected to purchase pressure-assist toilets with water velocity boosted by compressed air. They're noisier and costlier than gravity-assist models but are considered by many to be more effective at disposing of waste. Whatever kind of unit you choose, keep dental floss, feminine hygiene products, paper towels, baby wipes, and facial tissue out of the toilet; unlike bathroom tissue, they really aren't made to be flushed, no matter what the labels say.

To save the most money on a toilet, choose a basic gravity-assist two-piece model in white (sometimes available at the same cost in almond or gray), and keep a good toilet brush nearby. More effective pressure-assist flushing mechanisms, more color options, one-piece styling, elongated bowls, and 18-inch-tall bowls all add to the cost, so prioritize what matters most to you. At the high end, you'll find more designer color choices (including deep tones), pressure-assist flushing, and elongated bowls as standard; specially decorated motifs as part of a fixture suite; choices of handles in different materials and finishes; and unobtrusive push buttons on top of the tank.

A graceful, modern-style bathroom suite features a low-profile one-piece toilet and coordinating bidet, both wall-hung models, as well as a sculptural contemporary pedestal sink. Fixtures: Sottini.

Toilets can be had very economically, but if you're just redecorating and the toilet is in good shape, an attractive new wood or plastic toilet seat can make the whole fixture look almost new for just a few dollars. In a chilly house, some people swear by padded toilet seats, but skip those with embroidered butterflies or anything fussy. They're as un-chic as fluffy toilet tank covers.

BIDETS

Europeans consider the bidet ("bee-DAY"), a sit-down washbasin, a basic necessity for personal hygiene; for Americans, its function is often filled by frequent full-body baths and handheld showers. In the '80s, a bidet became a status element of the new, large American luxury bathroom, and today, most high-end bath fixture suites include a bidet, as do many midpriced suites. Looking somewhat like a toilet without a lid, a bidet requires its own water supply and drain and is usually installed along the same wall as the toilet, 30 to 44 inches away.

STEAM SHOWERS AND SAUNAS

Whether you like the high humidity of steam or the dry heat of a sauna, you can create a health club at home with one or both of these fixtures. A steam shower is easier: Install a self-contained unit, or convert your existing shower into a steam room. New shower modules with steam units often come with a lighted dome top, a timer, and a seat. If you convert an existing shower, make sure the door seals entirely before installing a steam generator, and if you have solid-surfacing or acrylic shower walls, make sure they won't be marred by the steam. You can tuck the machinery out of sight in a vanity.

To experience the dry heat of a sauna at home, you'll need a space at least 4×4 feet to create an enclosure that houses an electric heater topped with rocks (preferably igneous periodite). Water is ladled onto the hot rocks to produce humidity (but not steam), and soft, aromatic woods such as cedar or redwood are used for the walls and benches. Saunas are available in precut and prefab kits. Steam showers and saunas are not recommended for kids, pregnant women, or anyone with high blood pressure or heart trouble.

What could be better than a private toilet compartment that includes a matching bidet? Your own personal sauna in the bath, that's what! This luxurious space has both—and more.

Fittings: Go With the Flow

FITTINGS INCLUDE faucet handles and spouts, pop-up drains, trip levers for the toilet, mixing valves for the shower, hand sprays or other added sprays in the shower, outlets and controls in the whirlpool tub, and more. If your fixtures are in basically good shape and access is not a problem, you can do a lot to update the look of your bath just by replacing old fittings. New fittings tend to operate better, too. For instance, faucets with washerless construction are state of the art; those with ceramic disk cartridges inside are top of the line, usually needing no maintenance.

Iron faucet handles in the form of resting swans make distinctive companions for a decorative iron-and-marble vanity table and cast-iron sink. Fixtures and fittings: Kohler.

Fittings, sometimes called the "jewelry" of the bath, are among the most fun things to shop for. You have your pick of styles, from charmingly old-fashioned cross-handles to modern Eurostyle single-control units. For easy use and traditional or modern style, choose levers or, even easier, distinctive wrist-blade handles. Cross-handles and levers are available in wood or ceramic as well as metals to coordinate with the rest of your bath, but be careful about trying to match color tones: The white of the china sink may not match the white of ceramic handles.

Shower fittings are just as varied as those for sinks. Faucets may be single-handled for a modern look or have traditional separate hot and cold controls; the showerhead may be a drenching rosette or sunflower style or be adjustable, with a variety of stream intensities. For children or anyone who needs to shower sitting down, get a detachable showerhead on a height-adjustable slide bar that can be used in position or as a handheld shower. You can also install one or more shower bars with holes that produce streams at various heights along with a regular showerhead.

Many shower accidents occur when bathers slip trying to avoid an unexpected blast of too-hot water, so make sure your showerhead has a pressure-balancing valve, especially if children, the disabled, or older people will be using the unit. The valve prevents the sudden surge of hot water that occurs when someone else flushes a toilet or starts the washing machine. Pressure-balancing valves work in conjunction with a high-temperature stop (usually preset by the plumber) to prevent scalding.

Quality fittings often have a base of brass, but the finish may be brass, chrome, gold, pewter, ceramic, enamel, crystal, plastic, or what have you. If opulent gold fittings are in your budget, use a reputable supplier, and ask for the paperwork to be sure they're what the industry calls "heavy gold plating," which is anywhere from 13 to 50 millionths of an inch thick. If you like the golden glow but not the price, very recent developments in brass finishes give the first truly guaranteed tarnish-free brass. It's great with any style, particularly classical looks. Chrome's cool, shiny gleam is perfect for modern settings; for a softer look consider brushed nickel or elegant, traditional pewter. Ceramic and crystal may be contemporary or traditional; plastic and other novelty insets are usually modern.

What if you aren't replacing everything but want new brass fittings on your new fixtures? You can buy new brass fittings for all your fixtures, but if your existing fixtures have chrome fittings that are still in good shape, consider this: Remove the handles and clean any hard-water deposits that make them hard to turn, and shop for combination chrome-and-brass fittings for the new fixtures. The mixed-metal look is contemporary and chic. But whatever fittings you choose, look for vanity cabinet door handles and drawer pulls in the same materials and style to coordinate. Exception: when you discover some really special, whimsical pulls. Verdigris-bronze fish or pewter leaves may be just the artful touch your bath needs!

Above: *In a small bath or powder room, every detail counts, so this uniquely dramatic sink fitting—and eye-catching mirror in the same spirit—really stand out.*

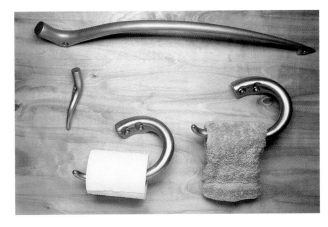

Cabinet door and drawer pulls and other hardware, the "jewelry" of the bath, offer a chance to express your design sense with striking or whimsical motifs in various metals and other materials. Manufacturer: Trout Studios.

Cabinets

CABINETRY DOESN'T PLAY the starring role in the bath that it does in the kitchen, but it's just as important. Function comes first, of course: Plan enough storage for everyone who uses the bathroom, and make sure vanity doors or cabinet drawers don't interfere with opening and closing the bathroom door. It's been known to happen!

Maximizing bath storage is key to keeping the place looking neat, so plan for ample storage space early in the remodeling process. Buy as spacious a vanity as will comfortably fit; recess tall, shallow shelving units (with or without doors) between wall studs; build in open shelves for colorful, neatly folded towels; or put a linen closet just outside the bathroom in the hall or in an adjoining master bedroom. If you're just redecorating this time, simply

Built-in drawers and clever pull-out "columns" hiding additional shelves offer lots of storage unobtrusively. A handsome washed finish enhances the discreetly elegant traditional style.
Cabinets: Rutt of Atlanta.

hanging a handsome shallow cabinet on the wall above the toilet can help ease the storage crunch. For items you don't mind keeping in view, narrow, tempered glass shelves with rounded corners are unobtrusive and useful.

In addition to doored cabinets, you can choose convenient storage drawers, swing-out hampers, and more. Most cabinet manufacturers make both kitchen and bath cabinetry, so you may want to see if any kitchen units have features you desire. Like kitchen cabinets, bath cabinets may be factory-made stock units, semicustom units that come in standard sizes but offer a choice of door styles or finishes, or custom-made units to fit your exact specifications. Whatever you choose, request self-closing cabinet hinges and self-closing doors to avoid accidents from doors and drawers left ajar.

When it comes to styles, you have a wide choice, from clean-cut modern units in carefree synthetic materials to opulent traditional designs in fine, furniture-grade woods. Proper ventilation and a waterproof finish are the secrets to using good-quality wood in the bathroom, so don't hesitate if that's your preference. Real wood cabinets make a warm, natural contrast to the predominantly colder materials used throughout the room. Wood on bathroom cabinets may be stained in a natural wood tone; given a colorwash stain; whitewashed with a bisque finish; painted with a waterproof, opaque paint; or given a faux finish to resemble marble or other material. If floorspace is really tight, paint or stain built-in cabinets and any freestanding pieces the color of the walls to minimize visual clutter. You can bring in additional hues with towels and accessories.

When selecting built-in cabinets, you can choose from "frameless," also called European-style, for a clean-lined, very modern look, or conventional framed cabinetry, which can look traditional or contemporary depending on the door style. For a modern look, choose a slab (plain panel) or channel (a horizontal groove or pull along the bottom) style. Select elegant cathedral (arched top panel) or curved raised panel for a traditional, formal look; for a traditional, country style, consider board and batten (a door made of narrow vertical boards). A square raised panel door can look either traditional or contemporary and can work well in a transitional-style bath.

The trend in recent years has been away from medicine cabinets and toward large wall-hung mirrors, but that solution begs the storage question. A big vanity may make an overhead cabinet unnecessary, but if you don't have one and don't want to skirt a pedestal or wall sink or bring in covered baskets or other storage, you will want to make room for a medicine cabinet.

A medicine cabinet mounted on the surface of the wall above the sink is an easy option, but for a better look, choose one the same width as, or a little narrower than, the vanity or pedestal sink itself, and select a frameless-looking unit with the mirror (beveled-edge is elegant) extending to the edge of the cabinet door. An arched-top mirror cabinet is a pleasing option that echoes the rounded shapes of bath fixtures.

If you're able to open up the wall, neater and more stylish than a surface-mount cabinet is a model hung in the recessed area between wall studs so that the mirrored surface is nearly flush with the

Furniture that looks, or really is, freestanding is a hot bath-style trend. This charming traditional hutch features ample open and closed storage for bath supplies and a wealth of period-style touches. Cabinets: Wood-Mode.

wall. If your vanity or sink is tucked into an alcove, you may want to mirror the back wall and recess a medicine cabinet into each side wall. If youngsters have access to the bath, be sure to install inexpensive childproof latches on any medicine chest and lower cabinet.

The freestanding furniture look that's so popular in kitchens is also a hit in the bath, so if you've got the room, bring in a chest of drawers or an armoire in the style of your bath. If that's too much for the available space, you might consider actually converting a chest into a vanity; drawers below the top one can stay functional. Simpler yet, you can add charm with a small wooden child's chair or stool to hold extra towels or with a basket holding rolled fingertip towels or loofah sponges. Don't overlook offbeat solutions: An artist's tabouret (a small cabinet on wheels with a multitude of shallow swing-out trays) is a fine place to store makeup and medicines in a house without small children.

Countertops

YOUR VANITY and any other storage units in the bathroom will need countertops, and the way they look can go a long way toward enhancing your decorating scheme. Many of the same materials used in kitchens are available for the bath.

Most economical are high-pressure, decorative laminates (not the same as low-pressure laminates such as melamine, which is often used for the fronts of modern-style cabinets). Laminates may have color on the surface or all the way through, and they come in an endless array of colors, patterns, and even textures. Consider plain white or almond that resembles high-end solid surfacing to visually expand the space and provide maximum decorating flexibility, or you can choose anything from luxurious faux malachite to fun 1950's boomerang motifs. Laminate is fairly durable, but if it is damaged, it's difficult to repair. Dark seams and edges are visible on the surface-color type; a rolled front edge avoids this.

Ceramic tile, a classic choice, is surprisingly affordable and ages gracefully. It's highly durable and impervious to water and comes in limitless colors, patterns, and textures. Plain stock tile in a light neutral or pastel color is inexpensive and can be perked up with coordinating hand-painted tiles along a wall border or around a mirror. (If you use plain-colored tiles, open all the boxes and mix the tiles up so that any variation in color won't be noticed.) More elaborate patterns, colors, and textures are costlier but equally durable. The grout between ceramic tiles may discolor or mildew: To solve this, specify a darker-toned grout, or have the tiles set very closely together.

Cultured marble usually is made of cast polymer with a gelcoat surface for durability and stain resistance. Economical and popular, it offers the convenience of an integral sink within the countertop.

Solid surfacing is made of different blends of polyester alloys, acrylic, crushed minerals, and other synthetic materials. Each brand uses different materials, but they're all seamless, very durable, and easy to repair. Solid surfacing is also great if you want an integral sink bowl that blends seamlessly with your countertop. Solid-surfacing material is costlier than laminate or ceramic tile but less expensive than natural stone.

Marble, granite, and other natural stone countertops are the most luxurious and expensive choice. They're extremely durable, but granite stands up to stains from alcohol and cosmetics better than marble does. Slate is an option—its natural layers make a pleasing texture—but all natural stone should be sealed to protect against stains and scratches. Don't try for more than a narrow overhang with natural stone: It's very heavy, and its own weight will cause it to break off. If you want a wider overhang, install corbels (well-anchored, heavy brackets) beneath each end for support. Natural stone is so beautiful, even a dramatic choice will probably please your next buyer, but remember that dark colors make a space look smaller. If your heart is set on marble but the cost is daunting, consider large (12-inch-square) marble tiles set closely together.

For a really unique and dramatic countertop, you can specify stainless steel, copper, concrete, or even wood (if it's redwood or cedar and waterproofed with a plastic finish). Be creative!

Virtually any material can be used to surface walls and floors in the bathroom as long as it's waterproof, either naturally or by means of an impervious finish. Wood-paneled walls and floors are rare because of the upkeep required, but if your bath is large, you may want to use wood outside the shower area. Wood window and door frames and doors are used just about everywhere; since they're painted or varnished, they withstand ambient moisture fairly well. A good ventilating fan is important in any bath, and in one with wood, it's essential. If you love wood but don't want the upkeep, investigate the new synthetic wood flooring materials. They're surprisingly realistic-looking and have all the waterproof benefits of a synthetic.

Ceramic tile, marble, and granite make handsome and highly durable flooring and wall surfaces for baths. Marble and granite tiles (slabs are too heavy) make a bath of unsurpassed luxury and beauty, and ceramic tiles go well on both floors and walls. Ceramic tiles that look antique, or like quarried stone, are now available. Glazed and crackled in earthy, stonelike textures, patterns, and colors, they resemble everything from tumbled marble to aged terra-cotta. Just be sure to use ceramic tiles made for flooring on the floor—wall tiles may look similar but aren't strong enough. And be certain to specify a nonslip surface on these floors. Some ceramic tiles have the low-luster, textured look of tumbled marble or other natural stones that makes them more slip-resistant. Smaller tiles with more numerous, thicker grout lines also improve traction.

Your choices don't end here. For a look that's both modern and rustic, consider cement flooring.

Today's synthetic wood flooring is remarkably durable and realistic-looking. Choose the look of traditional oak or pine, or indulge in a more exotic look like the burled wood shown here. Laminate flooring: Mannington.

Painted or stained, it's a dramatically different look, and the material is naturally waterproof and non-slip. Sheet vinyl or vinyl tiles are inexpensive and look better than ever these days: Top-quality lines do a nice job with faux-marble or faux-ceramic tile looks. Sheet vinyl avoids the potential problem of moisture seeping between tiles and loosening them, but vinyl tiles are quick and simple for anyone to install. Nonslip surfaces aren't really an option with vinyl flooring, so exercise care in wet areas.

Contoured or wall-to-wall bathroom carpeting has fallen out of favor for style and sanitation reasons, but the predominantly hard-surfaced bathroom can benefit from the soft texture of a rug or

Inventive glazing and crackling treatments give these ceramic tiles the depth and interest of antique tiles or quarried stone, lending an exotic air to a traditional bath.
Designer: Kim Bernard, ASID, Walker Zanger.
Tiles: Walker Zanger.

two underfoot. Just be sure to use rugs with nonslip coatings on back or use nonslip rug pads. Textured rubber tiles like those used in hospitals are fun for a modern bath or one used by kids, and they're nicely slip-resistant. Whatever type of flooring you choose, make sure it's installed over a clean, level, dry subfloor: This is one job you don't want to have to tear out and do over!

Bathroom walls in the shower area may be ceramic, marble, or granite tiles; solid surfacing; or laminate materials. For a space-expanding look, you can extend these materials to the rest of the bath or add interest with different wall treatments. A popular example is tile carried high on the shower wall that stops at the chair-rail level in the rest of the bath to be replaced by glass block, wood paneling, wallpaper, or paint.

Rather modern but undeniably beautiful, glass block can be used for interior walls, for half walls to create partitions without blocking light, or for exterior windows. If you love wood paneling, select the kind that has been treated with a waterproof plastic finish, and choose redwood or cedar, which withstand moisture better than other woods. If your choice is wallcovering, make sure it's vinyl, and use moisture-resistant adhesive not ordinary wallpaper paste. Paint is the most economical choice, so buy the best, and specify gloss or semigloss for easy cleaning and extra moisture resistance. Even with

waterproof surfaces, adequate ventilation is a must, so shop for a ceiling fixture fan or fan/light at the same time you shop for surfacing materials.

Veined, smoked, and tinted mirrors have fallen out of design favor since the '70s, but large-scale, clear mirrors are still an ideal wall surfacing material in the bath. They add glamour to a large space, make a small one look bigger, and brighten up any space by reflecting light from the usually minimal windows. To use large areas of mirror successfully, make sure it's hung properly (it's extremely heavy). Keep it out of shower areas because moisture seeping into the mirror's edges will ruin the silvering. And be sure you know what scene it will reflect! Many people prefer to mirror only the top half of the wall and use tile or other material below.

For a glamorous look, surround a frameless mirrored medicine cabinet with mirror, or hang an ornately framed mirror (Venetian glass framing is fabulous) on top of the large wall mirror. For an uninterrupted look, have any wall sockets on the mirror covered with mirror also. If your vanity counter is deep, the wall mirror may be too far away for putting on makeup, so plan for a portable, magnifying countertop mirror. Telescoping mirrors are a great idea for users of all heights.

Don't forget the door when planning your bath: To make the room usable for anyone, make sure the doorway is at least 32 inches wide, even if it's the powder room. If you're using a conventional door, it's better if it swings out than in; if someone has fallen, an inward-swinging door may be impossible to open. If floorspace is tight, consider a pocket door that slides into a slot in the wall or bifold doors that fold back against the wall.

Good lighting is as important in the bath as it is in the kitchen and even more often neglected. Think of all the delicate grooming and first-aid operations performed in the bathroom, and you'll realize why you should plan for adequate lighting early in your remodeling job. Electrical outlets and switches are easier to move than plumbing pipes if the wiring is reasonably accessible, and that one lone ceiling fixture isn't remotely OK!

Plan for maximizing natural light first: glass block or textured, frosted, or stained glass for eye-level windows in the wall; clear glass for a skylight if possible. For artificial light, plan on at least 4 watts of incandescent lighting per square foot (160 watts in a 5×8-foot bath or 280 watts in an 8×10-foot bath). If you choose fluorescent lighting, figure 2 watts per square foot. Incandescent lights and deluxe "warm white" fluorescents behind a diffuser are flattering; "cool white" fluorescents are not and should be avoided. Halogen lights are hot but yield a bright light from tiny sources. The new natural-spectrum lights are closer to sunlight than any other artificial source available, and many people feel these lights give the psychological health benefits of the real thing. Their bulbs are only slightly costlier than conventional incandescent bulbs.

For grooming, lights on both sides of the mirror are better than overhead, where they cast shadows. You'll need strong lighting over or around the mirror, but don't overdo it: If the mirror reflects the lights as it does with theatrical strip lighting, you'll get double the dazzle—and double the heat. For lighting above the shower area, be sure to use a fixture rated for damp areas. Over the bathtub, you may want lighting on a rheostat to make bright for reading or dim for relaxing. For general, ambient lighting, multiple recessed ceiling fixtures are the most efficient and neat-looking, but if you're not planning to redo the ceiling, you may opt for period lighting (simply styled is better) in a traditional space or track lighting in a modern one. Up-lighting sconces are also good choices for general lighting. Crystal-dripping chandeliers are great in a show-house bath, but for safety and an uncluttered look, you'll want to keep ceiling fixtures and wall sconces fairly unobtrusive. And don't forget, the most exciting lighting fixture in the world can't rival the spectacular effect of natural sunlight flooding a bath!

The spectacular overhead light fixture provides a burst of color to tie in the blue accents scattered throughout this bath. Subdued lighting overhead and on the mirror works here since the room gets plenty of natural light.

Modern Conveniences

AN OPEN WINDOW isn't enough ventilation to protect your bathroom wallcoverings, wood cabinets, and even your home's insulation, so put an exhaust fan on your must-have list early on. Fan-only units can be unobtrusive if you recess them into a soffit or ceiling; fan/light combinations are practical— you can choose from regular lighting or heat lamps. Once you've experienced a heat lamp after your bath or shower, you won't ever want to be without it! Kids and older people who feel the chill even more will really appreciate it, too.

A wall heater in the master bath and an infrared heat lamp located safely in the ceiling of a kids' bath will keep everyone toasty. For European-style pampering, consider a freestanding or wall-mounted towel warmer, either electrical or hooked to your home's hot-water heating system. If you've got the room, a fireplace in the bathroom is the most luxurious warming method of all. You don't need a conventional, built-in fireplace with a chimney, because several manufacturers offer ventless fireplaces that are convenient as well as romantic. Underfloor radiant heat, either electrical or from hot-water pipes in the floor, is another luxurious treat: Since heat rises, there are no chilly spots in the room. But whatever you do, don't even think about a portable space heater!

Beyond these basics, the sky's the limit for what your bath can include: a built-in TV with VCR, a state-of-the-art audio system to transport you while you soak, a telephone, or even a computer. A security system panel in the bath may be a good idea, especially for an older person who may need to summon help when others aren't at home. Shop the high-end design centers and shelter magazines, including those that specialize in home electronics. You may be inspired to cut a few corners elsewhere to budget for a convenience that didn't even exist a few years back!

A heat lamp in the bathroom is nice, but a fireplace is spectacular! Today's technology makes ventless, go-anywhere fireplaces possible, so you don't need a conventional built-in version.
Whirlpool tub: Jacuzzi Whirlpool Bath.

NONSLIP FLOORING, handrails or grab bars for tubs and showers, pressure-balancing valves on showerheads to protect against scalding, and tempered glass for shower doors are some of the safety basics your installer should consider nonnegotiable. Another, required by building codes, is a GFCI (ground fault circuit interrupter) for any outlet near a water source. If there's an electrical short, as in a hair dryer hitting the tub, a GFCI instantly shuts off the power.

Maintenance is inevitable in any bath, so make it easy. From the plumber's perspective, the best bath layout has the water supply and drain/waste/vent pipes all in one wall. One "wet wall" makes repairs easier. If, like many baths, yours has fixtures on two or three walls, do the next-best thing: Keep water lines and shut-off valves accessible in case you or a plumber needs to get at them. This includes whirlpool tubs installed into a tile-covered platform: Plan for a hatch that can be opened near the controls.

For day-to-day maintenance, make sure you really know how to clean those gold-plated faucets, marble counters, hand-painted sinks, and wood-paneled walls. They may be able to stand up to water but could be damaged by an all-purpose industrial cleaner with abrasives and bleach!

Safety was clearly a concern for this homeowner. Two custom-designed grab bars were installed for support as she enters and exits the tub; wrap-around safety rails near the toilet and a nonskid tile floor provide additional function and safety.

Bath Safety and Maintenance

Style Considerations

WHILE MANY PEOPLE abandon their home's signature style at the bathroom door, you don't have to. Every popular decorating style can be interpreted for the bath. On the other hand, the bath is one place you can indulge in styles that depart from those used in the rest of the house. So why not make your bath a romantic refuge or your kids' bath a tropical aquarium? You may even want to treat the powder room to a more adventurous or opulent look than in the rest of your home, indulging in ornate mirrors, lavish tile work, vividly colored wallcovering, or an unusual sink. Whatever styles you love, you're sure to find ideas worth adapting in these pages.

This bath shows off modern style at its best. Every element is designed with sinuous, simple forms that let the material star. Rounded shapes are safe as well as soothing. **Manufacturer: Sottini.**

Choosing Your New Look

To JUMP-START your bath style search, this section offers brief descriptions of about a dozen of the most popular design styles, with suggestions on how you might interpret them in your bathroom. Of course, it's easiest to create a whole new look if you're doing a total remodeling job, but even if you're not, take heart. Because the typical bath is fairly small, it only takes a few key elements, or even just new wallcovering borders and accessories, to suggest a new style in your bath. The trick is to decide on a color scheme and a visual theme and then use them consistently throughout the room. In these pages, you'll see baths that play it safe with all white or all beige fixtures and walls but let loose with some very expressive, imaginative colors and patterns in the less permanent elements. To create a coherent look, employ the decorating "rule of three," and repeat each major color in your setting at least three times.

What if you've created a cohesive style in the rest of your home and would like to extend it to the bath, but your budget won't go for a complete redo? Relax. Permanent elements that might not "go" with your home's overall look can adapt just fine, with a little imagination. One homeowner on a budget whose palette featured the English garden tints of celadon green and rose despaired of a master bath tiled in yellow—until she and her husband hit on a watercolor scheme of sand, violet, aqua, and lemon. The room became their "English Caribbean retreat." So keep an open mind as you look at your own bath and its possibilities!

Creativity in the bath is great, but you should consider a few practical points.

- **Never sacrifice safety for style.** Sharp-cornered cabinets, tubs reached by steps without handrails, floors and bath rugs that aren't slip-resistant—these prescriptions for disaster are totally avoidable, so don't settle. Insist on a bath that's as user-friendly as it is fabulous-looking.

- **Plan for the long term.** Consider using as many universal-design products and layout ideas as possible. If you're sinking a lot of money into the master bath of your dreams, you want to be sure you can enjoy it as your physical needs change through the years. The time to install reinforcement blocks for grab bars is before, not after, you reclad the walls in beautiful marble!

- **Keep it simple.** Some decorating looks tend to use more accessories, more busy fabrics…more of everything. Employ these looks if you love them, but edit rigorously. Too many tchotchkes and a riot of colorful, large-scale patterns will make the bath look small and cluttered.

When selecting accessories, remember all the stuff that naturally accumulates in a bathroom, and you'll probably want to keep the decorating clutter down. Preserve visual serenity with as much closed storage as possible unless you're neurotically neat. The neat, ordered open shelves in home-decorating magazines were set up for the photo shoot, not for the morning rush hour! (Make an exception for a pretty basket full of rolled hand towels or a shell full of usable-size scented soaps that further your color scheme.)

- **Deploy your dollars cleverly.** Ask your contractor for ways to keep costs down in areas that don't affect function, safety, or looks so you'll have more left to spend where it counts. "What counts" is different for everyone, so do what matters to you, not your mother or your neighbor. For example, if you can find the time, do as much tear-out as you feel competent to handle (and agree with your contractor about the dollar value of your labor so it doesn't show up on your bill). Consider a vanity made of large marble tiles, not a whole marble slab; a less fancy toilet, but one that offers pressure-assist flushing; or plain ceramic tiles in most places, accented by hand-painted ones for borders and backsplashes. You'll certainly come up with your own list of trade-offs that don't feel like sacrifices. Just be sure you don't sacrifice quality when it counts.

- **Demand the same quality and taste in bath accessories as you do for the rest of your home.** Just say no to the fluffy toilet seat and tank covers, skimpy contoured bath rugs, lace-and-moiré satin-trimmed toilet paper covers and tissue box holders, bas-relief resin wall art depicting old-time bathroom fixtures, and so on. These impulse items still beckon from every bazaar and highway gift shop, but there are many more chic and elegant ways to create a romantic look these days.

If you like a sleek, modern scheme, make sure the items you choose are made of heavyweight, top-quality acrylic, plastic, metal, or glass. Well-made acrylic accessories with the frosty, pastel look of sea glass are attractive; funky colored metal items with a 1950's drink set look are fun. In general, modern-style items designed and made in Italy, Sweden, Denmark, and the United States have a good track record at a variety of price points. Next best, and often much less expensive, are those designed in these countries but manufactured elsewhere. Modern often doesn't age well unless it's done well, so take time to get the details right.

Even if you have a glass-door or open-area shower that eliminates the need for a shower curtain, you'll have to contend with fabric in the bath in the form of towels, bath mats, and, most likely, bath rugs. Quality really counts here: Skip the ones with printed-on designs and colors that fade unevenly, and choose plain, solution-dyed colors and self-patterned designs achieved with permanent textures. Towels and rugs are major allies in furthering a color scheme. Watch for white sales, and stock up on necessities.

- **Don't get too cute with the kids' bath.** You'd love to give them a spectacular children's theme bath like the ones you see in the magazines. Go ahead, but confine the fantasy elements to things you can change fairly easily, such as wallcovering borders, not installed tiles. Choose timeless, gender-neutral colors you can pair easily with other tones (teal green goes as well with lilac as it does with navy blue), and mix in new patterns as children grow. Many people find they redecorate the kids' bath three times: when they're very small, when they're "big kids" in grade school, and when they're teens. And this same bath may become a guest bath later on! So choose permanent fixtures and surfacing materials with a long-range view in mind.

The following pages offer a wide array of traditional, contemporary, and transitional design looks and their signature elements in the bath. You're sure to find plenty of exciting ideas that can be adapted to your bath!

ANUMBER OF appealing looks can be found under the wing of traditional style. All have stood the test of time; one or more is just right for your home.

In general, traditional styles are more complex and symmetrical than contemporary styles. Pedestals on sinks are reeded with vertically striped depressions, bases appear to be separate and may have a different design, toilets are two-piece, and fittings and hardware (brass or pewter-look) are relatively ornate. A claw-foot tub and arched Palladian windows are icons of traditionalism.

At its best, traditional style—rustic or refined— evokes dignity, grace, and warmth. Happily, a few signs of wear just add to its heirloom patina. Traditional style doesn't come naturally to today's bath, since it's a relatively small space dominated by modern fixtures. But using timeless materials— ceramic tile, marble, fabric, porcelain, even wood— brings the spirit of tradition home.

Federal blue and linen white combine to make an elegant American country–style bath. A punched-tin insert on the upper cabinet is a classic country touch. Cabinets: StarMark Cabinetry, Inc.

AMERICAN COUNTRY

To bring the warm appeal of this style to your bathroom, avoid stark colors, especially black and white. Instead, go for a soft Navajo white, unbleached linen, or the tan of wheat for backgrounds. They're warm but not dark, so they'll flatter skin tones without making the bath seem smaller. For accent colors, choose antiqued tones: old rose, barn red, denim blue, or soft green.

A vanity in golden oak or Shaker-style maple with a plain, off-white ceramic or stone-look top and a white porcelain sink bowl works well, as does a traditionally styled pedestal sink. You may even want to investigate one of the new bowls that stand on top of the counter: One in white porcelain could

recall an antique washbowl. And don't forget a claw-foot tub for maximum nostalgia. For fixtures and hardware, skip the shiny chrome, and choose antiqued brass or a brushed-finish nickel for the soft look of old pewter. If you love wood and lots of it, consider naturally finished golden oak Shaker toilet seats and towel bars, but don't overdo it.

If you're shower-curtain shopping, keep country in mind. Most baths are a bit small for the riotous pattern of patchwork, but there's no reason why you can't enjoy a tablecloth-checked or mattress-ticking-striped fabric, or even a subtle plaid. Simpler yet, use plain, off-white muslin with a liner. Choose one or two colors from your fabric for towels, a bath mat, and a bath rug, or add another pattern with a simple rag rug in the same tones as your color scheme. Further the look by adorning windows with simple handkerchief-point valances; for more coverage, add café curtains or wood shutters. For soap dispensers and other accessories, choose pieces with the look of hand-thrown pottery or creamware. Handmade, round soaps and hand-embellished, well-ironed cotton or linen guest towels (available at many resale shops) are old-fashioned without being kitschy. Use natural or rustically painted wicker baskets or hampers for extra storage. If you've got the floor space, a small, Shaker-style child's chair heaped with rolled hand towels is a charming touch.

ENGLISH COUNTRY

Charming, comfy, and wonderfully romantic, English country style is one of the world's best-loved styles, as it has been since its Victorian heyday. More polished than American country style, the English look offers relaxed gentility with a touch of whimsy. To achieve this look, choose a traditional-style cabinet in a fine-grained wood—maple, cherry, or mahogany—crowned by a white marble (real or faux) countertop. If space is tight, choose a traditionally styled pedestal sink with a reeded column base and a curvy backsplash. Either way, select traditional brass or pewter-look fittings, as ornate as you like. Underfoot, small black-and-white ceramic tiles are classic. Consider adding a chair rail with board-and-batten walls below and a wallcovering with a garden motif (especially roses, violets, and ivy) above. If you've got a combination tub/shower or a claw-foot tub, curtain it with a colorful cotton chintz floral or crisp white cutwork curtains, and hang matching café curtains at the

window. For the soap dispenser and other accessories, china with a floral pattern in your color scheme is pretty. English country style blooms in fresh pastel colors: tea rose, cantaloupe, robin's egg blue, and buttercream paired with lettuce or celadon green. Choose a couple of these for your towels, soaps, and other accessories.

FRENCH COUNTRY

Charming French country is always in vogue. To create this romantic style, select a traditional pedestal sink with a reeded column base and a curvy backsplash, or choose a wood vanity cabinet, preferably in pecan or fruitwood, with cathedral-topped, raised-panel cabinet doors and "antique" brass pulls. Continue the look with a white porcelain sink with curvy brass or pewter-look fittings and a marble or faux-marble countertop. If you need extra storage, the French-born armoire is a great solution that follows the traditional look of

Beautiful yet restrained, this elegant bath shows its English country inspirations in the cheerful garden-colored plaid and the wallcovering border of rosy garlands. The whirlpool tub framed in classic columns is a happy marriage of old and new. Designers: Molly Korb, CKD, CBD, and Linda Panattoni, MK Designs.

Opulence in a small space distinguishes this elegant French-inspired bath. A quartet of traditional artworks, a shaded chandelier and sconce lamps, and a jewel-tone color scheme convey formality and charm.

freestanding furniture. For color and practical beauty, terra-cotta floor tiles evoke the warmth of Provence, while hand-painted wall tiles and murals celebrate French artistry. For a shower curtain, choose a traditional Provençal print in cheery yellow, royal blue, and brick red; add a romantic balloon shade in a matching or coordinating print at the window. For a romantic color scheme, take inspiration from the palettes of French Impressionist or Expressionist paintings, perhaps in vibrant yellow-green, violet-blue, and coral cut with white. For accessories, choose Provençal-inspired hand-painted pottery and ornately curved wrought iron.

18TH CENTURY

If you're seeking a no-fail recipe for timeless elegance, this handsome, refined look borrows elements from several historical American and English styles. Based on 18th-century designs that express consummate symmetry and grace, this look includes Queen Anne, Sheraton, curvy Duncan Phyfe, and Chippendale styles from the golden age of furniture design. Your 18th-century setting may also include later influences, from French Empire to early English Victorian.

Start with heirloom-quality maple or cherry vanities with cathedral-topped, raised-panel doors and Chippendale-style brass hardware. (For a lighter 18th-century look, choose a vanity from the same period but in antiqued white, perhaps with painted or gilded embellishments.) Top cabinets with real or faux-marble countertops, and drop in pure white or hand-painted porcelain sinks in a traditional or scallop-shell shape, or find similarly styled pedestal sinks. Add traditionally styled, heavy brass fittings and accessories featuring neoclassical elements such as scallop shells and laurel leaf wreaths. Tapestry and moiré-look wallcoverings and window treatments are appropriate and are now available in water-tolerant materials. They're handsome in muted jewel tones (old gold, blue-green, Federal blue, burgundy, and old rose), and they're lovely and fresh in the cameo-pale tones of tea rose pink, primrose yellow, celadon green, sky blue, and white. Either way, you'll find the pedigreed look of 18th-century style gracious and wonderfully timeless.

Cabinets in rich cherry with cathedral-style doors express the dignity of 18th-century style. The traditional floral wallcovering lends a light-hearted feel, balancing the dark woods. A Palladian window is the crowning touch. Cabinets: Yorktowne Cabinets.

Border tiles in the ancient Greek key motif and corbel-style supports for the sink are among the many classical references in this Italian villa–style bath. An airy Aegean-blue-and-white color scheme is warmed by luxe touches of gilt.

ITALIAN VILLA

A spacious, luxurious bath seems made for Italian villa style. Inspired by the palatial yet airy homes of aristocrats from the time of the ancient Roman Empire to the opulent Renaissance, this style is luxurious but never heavy-handed. To create such a masterpiece, it's best to start with an impressive shell: generously scaled Palladian windows; arched doorways; and high ceilings. Continue with other grand gestures, including ornately carved vanity cabinets in fine-grained hardwoods embellished with ornate, antiqued brass hardware.

For surrounding surfaces, why not evoke the spirit of a Roman bath? Italy is one of the world's finest sources of quarried stone and artisan-made tiles, so indulge in luxurious natural stone flooring, countertops, backsplashes, and even entire walls, especially in a walk-in shower area. You can choose luxurious polished marble; durable, dramatic granite; interesting tumbled marble tiles; or hand-painted Italian tiles (or several of the above) to carry out your color scheme and decorating theme. Choose a hand-painted porcelain sink or one in a suite of fixtures, perhaps in a regal tone such as maroon, hunter green, eggplant, warm gold, or ivory. If the budget allows, consider a pedestal sink that's a work of art itself in agate or rose quartz. For fittings, choose ornately designed, elegantly traditional brass or pewter, perhaps with faucet handles adorned with quartz or another semiprecious stone.

Call on faux-finishing artists to conjure up the richly antiqued look of an ancient palazzo with richly dimensional plaster walls, sponged or painted with fresco scenes. Accent with faux-bois woodwork finishes, and, if you've always yearned for a bit of opulent gilding, feel free to indulge your Midas touch here. For the crowning effect, you may even commission a custom mural depicting the Tuscany countryside, a Roman temple ruin, or a Renaissance still life.

LODGE/CABIN

Get away from it all without leaving home in a rustic lodge/cabin-style bathroom. If you don't live in a log house, have a trompe l'oeil artist paint the "logs" on your walls, or, simpler yet, surround yourself with a palette of earth tones: greens,

Rustic stone creates a subtly dramatic frame for the tub and window area in this lodge-style bath. To keep natural tones from becoming too bland, inject a spirited color like the red in this striking ethnic-patterned rug.
Builder: Alpine Log Homes.

browns, and tans, accented with autumn-leaf colors of terra-cotta, brick red, and gold. Choose a vanity in a rustic wood such as oak or knotty pine, and add a simple sink, perhaps a bronze, pewter, or white porcelain bowl that sits entirely on a countertop of slate, tumbled marble, or other textured, rustic surfacing material. A claw-foot tub with an old-fashioned "sunflower" shower fixture and an unbleached muslin curtain would be fun in this room, but a plain walk-in shower tiled in tumbled marble would work equally well. Keep window treatments simple: stained wood shutters, Roman shades of plain muslin, or café curtains of homespun green-, brick-, or gold-and-white checks. Keep metals matte (choose antiqued bronze-brass, pewter, or brushed nickel; not shiny brass, chrome, or stainless steel) and accessories in wood or stoneware colored to blend with your palette.

SOUTHWESTERN

A bilingual blend of dramatic colonial Spanish and Native American influences, this is a look that offers timeless warmth and heritage for many homeowners, especially those in the Southwest. Frame the look with off-white plaster walls and exposed, dark-wood beams. A rustic, darkly stained wood vanity with wrought-iron-look fixtures and hardware fits right in with this style. For contrast, choose countertops in off-white tumbled marble, solid surfacing, or laminate. Terra-cotta tiles make a handsome floor, and colorful Spanish tiles recall cooling courtyard fountains—great around your spa tub! Against the dark woods and white walls, choose accessories, shower curtains, and window coverings in desert tones of soft coral and gray-green, or create a bright, happy mood with shades

in porcelain with hand-painted Mediterranean-inspired motifs are available. For beautiful, durable countertops, you can't do better than the ceramic tiles for which Italy, Spain, and Portugal are world-famous. Choose your color scheme—perhaps the classic royal blue, sun yellow, and white—and create a work of art with decorative tiles on your vanity countertop and backsplash. For walls, try the eye-catching combination of heavily textured plaster or stucco walls inset here and there with a jewel of a ceramic tile. For soap dishes and other accessories, choose from a wealth of Mediterranean hand-painted pottery and the characteristic blue- and green-tinged heavy glassware of the region. If your window's very sunny, fill it with fragrant lavender or rosemary, and top with a sail-white Roman shade.

of serape-inspired sunny gold, turquoise, brick red, yellow, and cobalt blue. Add baskets and, if your bathroom window has a sunny exposure, terra-cotta pots of cooling aloe vera plants.

MEDITERRANEAN

Italy, Spain, and Portugal are home to many of the world's most wonderful designs in stone and tile, while southern France and Greece each contribute a distinctive aesthetic of their own. Taken together, these rich cultures offer inspiration for any size bath. Mediterranean style includes freshly creative ideas in a context that's historically honored. It is a style that is also hearty and practical and makes an art of life's little pleasures. To get the look, choose a vanity cabinet in oak or pine (or, even more refined, in fruitwood or pecan) with antiqued brass fixtures and hardware. Sinks in hammered brass or

Far Left: *The soothing tones of desert rose, sandy tan, and tawny brown make a pleasant palette for this lovely Southwest-inspired bath.* Designers: Joe McDermott and Diane Wandmaker, CKD, Kitchen Studio. Cabinets: Hallmark. **Left:** *Nothing evokes the spirit of Mediterranean style like a wealth of intricately designed tiles. This classic quatrefoil pattern and its companion border design are set off by larger plain tiles that pick up tones from the patterned tiles.*

ALL THE GLORIES of ancient regimes seem gathered in this masterpiece of a bath. Motifs born in classical Greece and popular again in the Empire period of Napoleon resound throughout this spacious, luxurious room. While adhering to a subdued scheme of ivory, silver, gold, and brown, this bath is anything but austere. Evoking an opulent villa of yore, the room gives every element the royal treatment with mosaic inlays, frescoed murals, gilding, faux finishing, and much more. Among the room's many marvels, the soaking tub alcove reigns supreme, overlooked by a contemporary interpretation of a classical scene. No area is left unadorned. The marble floor in an ivory-and-taupe sunburst pattern is further embellished by a center medallion of laurel sprays. Overhead, a barrel-vaulted ceiling is faux finished in golden tones and a sunburst motif. Carefully chosen fine furniture and decorative accessories complete the regal look.

Above: *Set in its own shallow alcove and embellished with gilt and silver, this Empire-period writing desk makes a perfect vanity table. A Romantic period landscape and a mix of silver and golden-hued accessories are all that's needed to complete the picture.*

Opposite: *A more dramatic setting for a soak could hardly be imagined. A grand fresco of a contemporary beauty in a timeless setting provides a stunning background. Classical urns, lyres, and other motifs are rendered in silver on fine mahogany wood surrounding the tub. Even the floor is a sunburst of marble inlaid with mosaic laurel wreaths for today's conquering hero.*

Right: *An ebony-hued statue of an ancient Egyptian seems to guard the doorway to the separate compartment that houses the toilet and bidet. An Empire-inspired lingerie chest, a statue of a dog that seems plucked from some Gothic castle, and other opulent touches give this utilitarian space exceptional presence.*

A custom vanity features a lighted swivel mirror and jewelry dividers plus space for a TV and radio and hooks for a hair dryer and curling iron. Lingerie drawers and pull-out clothes and trash hampers help keep clutter under wraps. Cabinets: Rutt Custom Cabinetry.

A NEW MASTER SUITE in a handsome home, circa 1922, is a quietly luxurious retreat. A wealth of quality surfacing materials and intelligent design touches makes the space wonderfully livable as well as beautiful. Safety was important from the start to these homeowners, so grab bars were secured on each side of the tub; the tub deck was kept clear of fittings for easy, seated entry; and a textured, nonskid ceramic tile floor and a built-in solid-surfacing bench were installed in the shower. Custom cherry cabinets feature a beaded design on the door and drawer fronts that is elegant without being ostentatious. On the upper cabinets, glass-mullioned doors are curtained in pure white sheers for an airy, vintage look that keeps personal items out of sight. Open shelving shows off silver miniatures and favorite photos, while keeping towels handy.

Opposite: *The toilet is housed in a separate room with its own storage to keep the vanity and bathing area clutter-free. To create an extra-spacious look, the honed, tumbled-marble floors were installed on the diagonal.* Designer: Jere Bowden, CKD, Rutt of Atlanta. Tub: Aqua Glass; tub deck: DuPont Corian; sinks and fittings: Kohler.

Left: *A knotty pine vanity and the tub surround with a weathered washed finish blend quietly into the creamy walls of this Southwest-inspired bath with a spectacular view. Huge floor tiles in a rustic red-brown tone ground the space; the roughly hewn tub surround and vanity top add more important textural notes.*

A BATH in a vacation home, especially one with great vistas all around, seems made for the kind of sculptural, timeless design these two rooms exhibit. While the materials are ageless, their strong, simple good looks, relying more on texture than on artifice, create a rather contemporary mood. The mix is one of free-spiritedness, but with a certain comfort. In one bath here, weathered wood, rough-cut stone, and strategically placed beams work together to create a simple, striking room. In a space like this, a great view easily takes on the starring role. In the other bath, rounded, playful architecture and some carefully placed niches for classical reference lend a fresh look to exposed brick and other rustic elements. In this setting, whimsical accents and freestanding furniture add to the rich yet unassuming look. There are all kinds of comfort, and these baths illustrate just how easy to live with—and how sophisticated—rustic style can be.

Streamlined modern fixtures like this sink and toilet have a timeless sculptural look when set against natural materials. The decorative stones on the floor, the toilet compartment, the display niches, and a number of other elements repeat the softly curved forms of the fixtures in a pleasing way. For balance, exposed bricks and tiles with the look of tumbled marble add squared-off contrast.

IF YOU'RE LONGING for a more colorful bath but don't want it to get garish, adapt some of the design-savvy tactics used in abundance here. First, choose a trio of colors in approximately the same intensity: Fuchsia pink, mint green, and buttercup yellow create an exuberantly pretty scheme in this generously sized bath. Although the colors are bright, they're also soft, and because they're actually a variant of the complementary red-violet-and-yellow-green scheme, they're happily harmonious. Next, mix your core colors liberally with neutrals: Here, the room's many wood, terra-cotta, and white tones have a mellowing effect. Then, follow through with your core colors and neutrals in accessories: An ornate gilt-framed mirror, tortoiseshell bamboo baskets, and simple terra-cotta topiary pots all mix with surprising ease in this bath, thanks to their related golden tones. Finally, make sure your accessories carry through the spirit of your scheme: In this case, a mix of the grand and the garden-inspired creates a confident, romantic mood.

Left: *Board-and-batten paneling on the walls enhances this bath's charming vintage air. A semienclosed toilet compartment is a nice touch perfectly in keeping with the gracious mood of the space.*

Opposite: *A wire baker's rack makes an airy yet substantial storage piece comfortably heaped with colorful towels and earthy accents. The traditionally styled double-sink vanity cabinet has the look of a freestanding sideboard.*

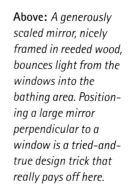

WHEN PRIVACY is not a problem, why not let the sun shine in? This spacious bath sees the light from every angle via a row of casement windows and a good-size skylight in the coved ceiling. To make the most of this lambent quality, the room's design celebrates the contemporary love of open spaces and clean surfaces, which are mostly pale marble and light-toned wood. Details, however, are gracefully traditional: Golden brass fittings and hardware gleam like jewelry against pale neutral surfaces. A pair of Art Deco–inspired wall sconces mounted directly on the vanity mirrors provides a deft transition between old and new and subtly alludes to the pale-toned glamour so well expressed in the Art Deco period. The color scheme of this bath—creamy ivory, hunter green, and taupe—is restful without being dull. For a master bath retreat, the effect is ideal: soothing yet sophisticated.

Opposite: *A wall filled with easy-to-operate, uncurtained casement windows gives bathers a room with a view while they soak and relax. (If your lot isn't quite this secluded, bottom-up pleated shades would create the same effect but offer privacy.) A state-of-the-art shower features a multistation handheld showerhead plus additional fixed spray sources.* **Designer: Fairhaven Design.**

Above: *A generously scaled mirror, nicely framed in reeded wood, bounces light from the windows into the bathing area. Positioning a large mirror perpendicular to a window is a tried-and-true design trick that really pays off here.*

Right: *Lovely traditional cabinetry is distinguished by subtle detailing and a mellow, honey-hued finish. Large mirrors, handsomely framed, reflect sunlight from the row of windows by day and the light from sconces and recessed fixtures overhead. Generously sized white porcelain sink bowls and heavyweight, gleaming fittings are quietly luxurious.*

WELL-TO-DO young Englishmen of the 18th and 19th centuries traditionally were sent abroad to France, Greece, and Italy to expand their cultural horizons before settling down. The souvenirs they brought home, back in the days before laws protected antiquities, were incomparably rich and precious, an atmosphere captured in this bath. The generously scaled space evokes the cozy opulence of an old English library and transports these homeowners to a place of elegance and supreme restfulness. Wrapped in ashes of roses, sage green, mahogany brown, and other deep tones favored in Victorian England, this bath seems a world away from the bright white modern era. Layer on layer of luxurious touches abound: marble flooring with mosaic insets depicting ancient themes; upholstered-and-fringed seating; silky, fringed draperies; an antique vanity with gilded legs; a gilt-and-ebony Empire-era vanity chair; a hand-painted mural; and more. What keeps the design from being too much of a good thing? A restrained color palette and carefully researched details.

Above: *A hand-painted mural that could have been painted in the 17th or 18th century is a handsome focal point above the tub, beautifully enclosed in furniture-grade wood paneling and marble. A stylized border of golden waves atop a green-on-green striped wallcovering maintains the subtly opulent color scheme.*

Right: *Ancient architectural drawings, plainly framed, embellish the alcove enclosing the toilet and bidet. An adjacent, separate shower compartment utilizes more of the dark green marble that covers the floor. Recessed lighting fixtures add drama to the scene, while traditional lamps and light fixtures enhance the romantic ambience.*

Opposite: *Handsome windows with Gothic Revival divided lites and frames that evoke neoclassical columns demand the best in window coverings. Here, bottom-up pleated shades provide privacy, while fringed, full-length draperies offer opulence. An antique vanity table and a chaise longue upholstered in ashes of roses seem perfectly at home next to the double-sink vanity.*

THE CABIN/LODGE LOOK is one of the easiest to abuse, but this savvy little space doesn't fall for the usual temptations. Details make the difference between a cabin-style bath that's too cute and one that's just right, like this one. Lots of black and white, a great foil to the variety of soft wood tones used in the room, injects a spirit that's sophisticated, young, and sharp. Where brushed nickel would give an appropriately aged, pewter look to the hardware, these homeowners chose shiny chrome in Victorian styles for a much punchier look without breaking character. Banker's drawer pulls in particular recall the silvery concha buckles of the old Southwest. Bead-board panels on the vanity, windows framed with simple white ruffled curtains, and a few tongue-in-cheek decorative accessories create a cabin-style bath that would work just as well in the suburbs or the city.

Victorian-style hardware is in keeping with an Old West look of the same vintage while adding needed sparkle to the scene. The guest towel discreetly echoes the moose motif of the wall border (see photo on opposite page) without overdoing it, while the wonderfully curvy soap dish/drinking glass unit adds an inventive touch. Glass jars used for canning, with their natural blue-green tint, make for simple yet decorative bath storage.

Hefty helpings of jet black, bright white, and silvery chrome keep this woodsy bath from becoming bland. The old-fashioned two-piece toilet and claw-foot tub are just two of the nostalgic elements that make this little bath fun. The border of moose and fir trees adds a humorous touch without being corny.

Leaded glass, textured in some places, stained in others, is enjoying a new vogue as a great way to let light into a bath while preserving privacy. Its faceted design is echoed in the various lace and cut-work accents around the room, for a look that's pretty but not fussy.

TRADITIONAL BATHS are perfect places to show off linens with a history—or pieces that just look that way. Fingertip towels, embellished with lace and embroidered cutwork, give any bath a pristine, elegant air. While genuine old lace and linen is very delicate, you can still enjoy it peeking out of a small drawer or festooning a small window as a casual valance. If you didn't inherit any of these treasures, poke around antique shops: You may find affordable pieces in less-than-perfect condition that have usable sections to sew onto new towels or decorate shelf-fronts. For more lavish use, save the heirlooms and look for imported or machine-made pieces. For the richest look, skip the synthetic lingerie-type lace in strong colors, and choose eyelet or Battenberg lace in crisp cotton. Virtually any color is flattered by a few lace accents, and there's no easier way to give a bath a fine bit of romance.

A floral wallcovering border in white and blue helps relate this bath's many delicate lace pieces and the strong, cobalt-painted walls. An austerely simple storage piece gets a softening effect thanks to lace shelf trim, while stock fingertip towels look pretty with sewn-on lace embellishments.

A wall-hung toilet and bidet can be accessed from a wheelchair if need be; a custom support rail is good-looking and functional. Cabinets: Wood-Mode; countertop: DuPont Corian; toilet and bidet: American Standard; ventilation unit: Broan.

THIS 1950S-ERA bath received a complete makeover to update its looks and to help its owner contend with the effects of multiple sclerosis. She specified a room that was accessible but not institutional-looking; a room that reflected the richly simple Arts & Crafts–inspired design, with its subtle Asian influences, that she had used throughout her home. The solution is an admirable example of universal access within a sophisticated decorative scheme. From up-to-the-minute features that offer safety and performance to Asian antiques that enrich the overall look, this bath is filled with thoughtful elements. Annexing two feet of extra width from an adjacent closet allows for the separate bathing and showering functions safety experts recommend. Grab bars and rails—some stock, some custom—are everywhere you'd want them to be but don't appear intrusive. An Asian-inspired wallcovering with a soft metallic finish gives depth and interest to the walls and ceiling. The result is a room that is universally appealing as well as universally accessible.

Opposite: *A whirlpool tub sub-mounted to a solid-surfacing platform eliminates the obstruction of a tub lip. Other features include grab rails for safety and lever-handled faucets for easy manipulation.* Designer: Rebecca Gullion Lindquist, CKD, CBD. Whirlpool: Trajet; whirlpool fittings: Kohler; glass block: Corning; wallcovering: F. Schumacher & Co.

A spectacular Venetian glass mirror takes pride of place above the dressing table and enhances the already sparkling atmosphere of the room. Roman shades and a simple straight-legged table, both in vanilla, let the mirror really shine.

WONDERFULLY SPACIOUS, light and bright, this traditional bath makes good use of every graceful design aesthetic possible. Tall, slender columns and carefully chosen antiques, furniture, and accessories create an impressive room that just happens to be a bath. But it's the abundance of mirrored and glassed surfaces, including a dazzling Venetian vanity mirror, that makes this space so captivating. With this much room to work in, a designer might be tempted to take the look over the top, but in this space, a composed air is maintained throughout. For example, some would have framed the very decorative Venetian glass mirror with fringed damask draperies and a gilded, heavily carved vanity table. Instead, faced with a mirror of such importance, the designer wisely kept the vanity table itself and the flanking windows' shades beautifully plain. It's this character of restraint that makes the best of today's traditional style so livable.

Above: *An opulent Art Nouveau–inspired ceiling fixture adds a glamorous note to the semienclosed compartment housing the toilet and bidet. The antiqued metal bath, enclosed in marble, is a classical allusion that also conducts heat to keep bathwater warm longer.*

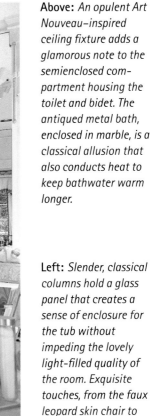

Left: *Slender, classical columns hold a glass panel that creates a sense of enclosure for the tub without impeding the lovely light-filled quality of the room. Exquisite touches, from the faux leopard skin chair to the mirrored antique storage cabinet, bespeak elegance from the past.*

The timeless beauty and dignity of China comes home in this exceptional powder room. The vanity, a spectacular inlaid chest, holds a sink bowl that rests completely on top of the vanity surface. Wallcovering recalls classic Chinese screen paintings of misty mountain scenes. Wallcovering: FSC Wallcoverings.

A POWDER ROOM is the perfect place to indulge your fantasies about long-ago times or faraway places. In spaces this small, great ideas can often be rendered without breaking the bank. An inventive example is the gold-and-cobalt-blue powder room designed like a miniature version of a 19th-century library. The window treatment (lined fabric with the look of Italian endpapers), the strongbox side table, and the library ladder all reinforce the literary look. The ivory-and-taupe powder room conveys the quiet elegance of aristocratic, ancient China. Whatever locale or era you'd like to recall in your powder room, do some research first. Get the color scheme down right with materials appropriate to the look you're seeking. Choose accessories with care to reinforce the style, and use just enough of them to make your design statement, no more. After all, what your guests want most in a powder room are proper function and scrupulous cleanness.

Opposite: *Some folks coyly call the bathroom "the library," but this gold-and-cobalt-blue powder room takes the look literally. Books, real and faux, cram the space with a colorful yet aristocratic look. There's just enough room for the faux-marble toilet and the diminutive sink, opposite.*

IF YOU LOVE the pale pink of English cabbage roses, the celadon of Asian porcelain, or a color drawn from a signature piece of some other culture, why not use it to develop your new bath's color scheme? An inlaid Japanese jewelry box was the inspiration for this room, filled with a wealth of style and amenities. Who'd guess this lavish family-size master bath was once a small bath and studio? In addition to making a distinctive personal statement, this bath is a clever example of the power of color. Warm, earth-tone marble makes the space as visually cozy as a wood-paneled library, without sacrificing the cool gleam the luxurious stone provides. Drawing once again on inspiration from the East, the home-owners chose a color palette of ebony, ivory, and cinnabar—the dark red-orange color of an ancient Asian lacquer. (A fine example of the painstaking craft is visible on the vase tucked into one of the storage shelves.)

Above: *Marble in rich, earthy tones creates a visually warm environment, sparked by ivory, black, and cinnabar red accents. Even the magazine rack maintains the mood.* Fixtures and fittings: Alsons, Grohe, and Kohler.

Left: *The mother-of-pearl-inlaid jewelry box that inspired this handsome bath looks right at home on the black double-sink vanity countertop. A row of brass-and-glass mirror sconces illuminates the scene without disturbing the masterfully simple look of the space.* Cabinets: Rutt Custom Cabinetry; lighting fixtures: Lighting by Leader.

Opposite: *Tiny "running lights" in tubes surround the tub's marble base, creating a fun, romantic ambience at night.* Designer: Janine Jordan, CKD, IIDA, IDS, JJ Interiors. Architect: John M. Eide, Jr.

An elaborately carved antique walnut mirror and a small chest are heirloom treasures that add richness and importance to this pretty little bath. A small wood footstool covered in pink damask adds a luxurious, feminine note of warmth; colors are picked up in the pale ribbons-and-flowers rug.

A PORTRAIT often adds a human, sentimental charm to a room, so why not include one in that most personal of rooms, the bath? Don't worry if it's not a family heirloom: You can find affordable, endearing portraits of people (real and imaginary) in antique stores and flea markets around the country. These poignant images of an idealized time gone by bring a special depth and richness to any bath. When you add a few carefully chosen pieces of "real" furniture in tones that echo those in your portrait, you may be surprised at how substantial even a tiny white bath can look. Victorian plant stands, wood-framed mirrors, lightly scaled footstools, end tables, nightstands, and wall curio shelves are all good options to add style without hogging the floor. If your bath furniture items are genuinely old pieces, consult an expert for maintenance tips. With care, your vintage bath will charm for many more years to come.

Opposite: *A vintage print of a farm girl is an important element in this charming little bath. It establishes the unabashedly sentimental mood and also helps relate the dark walnut furniture pieces to the mostly white setting.*

Most lodge-look rooms are soothing retreats in earthy tones of green, brown, and gold. These baths, however, rewrite the history books with a fearless use of knock-out color, especially bright red and cobalt blue. Surprisingly, these colors work just fine with the predominantly golden tones of the wood, creating a nicely balanced triadic scheme of the three primary colors: red, yellow, and blue. In addition to courageous color, these rustic beauties share a use of practical surfacing materials. In one bath, floors are wood like the walls, wrapping the whole space in golden tones. In another, white ceramic floor tiles are easy to clean and offer visual refreshment, too. In rooms this naturally dramatic, a few decorative accessories exhibiting influences from colonial Spanish to Southwest Native American are all the spark these schemes need. The effect is a tribute to the romance of the Old West, rejuvenated with a bracing jolt of contemporary flair.

Above: *Tucked into a discreet corner, the one-piece toilet in this bath is given a measure of privacy by the double-sink vanity. The vanity cabinet, simply crafted in rustic knotty pine, is topped by deep cobalt blue ceramic tiles that are as handsome as they are practical. Rosy red wallcovering and a Spanish-inspired mirror add sparkle and warmth.*
Builder: Rocky Mountain Log Homes.

Opposite: *A vintage-style tub in bright crimson red sets a confident tone for this one-of-a-kind bath. While contemporary, the glass-block panel evokes the small window panes of old, especially when it's set into a wall paved in fieldstone. Nearby, a comfy sofa in royal blue sets off the golden-hued log walls.*
Builder: Rocky Mountain Log Homes.

Left: *A sink alcove in a cheerful blue-striped wallcovering gets an extra punch of color from a red vanity, its paint agreeably scuffed and distressed for an aged look. Underfoot, a wildly modern rag rug in blue and red reinforces the whimsical look of the curly iron-framed mirror.*
Builder: Rocky Mountain Log Homes.

Above: *A fireplace in the bathroom? If you've got the space, why not? Glossy ceramic tiles with white grout around the hearth echo the teal-and-white color scheme. A hardwood floor is an unexpected look but perfectly logical in this gracious space.*

A KING-SIZE BATH takes to large expanses of deep or bright colors without becoming claustrophobic. In this room, deep blue-green distinguishes a spacious room done in elegant 18th-century style. A subtly striped wallcovering is classic, and its rich yet cool tones of teal balance the large amounts of pristine white used on the cabinets, tub surround, and window frames. Against the teal, sparkling mirrors and golden frames and hardware gleam, relieving any sense of darkness. Accents in raspberry, carried out in the floral rug, upholstered vanity chair, and flower arrangements, inject a note of warmth. This room is large enough to accommodate lots of extra bells and whistles: a separate room for the shower stall, toilet, and bidet on one side of the tub/vanity area; two large separate vanities; and even a fireplace. Not every room is this big, but the elegant decorating scheme would make a handsome impression in even a moderately spacious bath.

A tub enclosure that echoes the look of traditional raised-panel cabinet fronts integrates the luxurious tub into its 18th-century-style surroundings. Since privacy is not a problem, these large double-hung windows can be left unadorned. A few judiciously chosen accessories—topiaries, outsize ginger jars, framed architectural prints—are in character.

A gold-decorated sink beneath a gilt-framed mirror keeps company with an adjacent dressing table area and its own lavishly gilded mirror. Raised-panel cabinets, gold-plated fixtures, and elaborate candelabra sconces complete the aristocratic look. The plain walls and simple, traditional cabinets keep all that glitter from going over the top.

For the ultimate in soothing freshness, no color combination beats green and white. Perennially popular, it works everywhere in the home, and, unlike the more expected blue-and-white combo often used in bathrooms, a green-and-white scheme is seldom chilly. In both of these bathrooms, small amounts of green have an important impact. To carry out their traditional schemes, both rooms employ pedestal sinks (in one, the sink stands on a base to accommodate a tall user); tubs and showers with exposed pipes; and wood shutters on the windows, either painted white or finished in natural oak. Both rooms are mostly white, with a few touches of natural brown and green as accents. For a much more enclosing but equally appealing effect in a large bath, walls could have been painted a medium-dark green.

Old-fashioned bead-board paneling and classic reeded column-based pedestal sinks create a subtle striped effect while enhancing the vintage charm of this bath. Oversize white floor tiles set on the diagonal make the space look bigger.

Opposite: *Fern-sprigged wallcovering sets the mood of a quiet woodland glen in this spacious vintage-style bath that's predominantly pristine white. Handsome windows framed in oak with 18th-century bull-nose corner blocks and coordinating wood shutters further the link with nature in a refined way.*

This dressing table has all the presence of a grand china cabinet or armoire thanks to a wealth of handsome details. Gothic-arched, glassed cabinet doors are curtained inside to provide maximum storage with privacy.

Lᴵᴋᴇ ᴀ ꜱᴇᴛᴛɪɴɢ straight from some 19th-century French novel, this bathroom seems born for pampering a hero or heroine who will step out into the most romantic occasions imaginable. The room is so fully realized, it comes almost as a surprise that it is, indeed, a bathroom of today. The marble-surrounded soaking tub is dramatic in itself, but it's the setting—a beautiful bay window with true divided-lite panes and an abbreviated but just-right brocade window treatment—that really sets the tone. Throughout the room, other opulent details distinguish each element of this bath. On the vanity, an ogee-edged marble slab tops lower cabinets embellished with bull-nose and reeded column details that add 18th-century elegance. A richly colored painting in an ornate gilt frame is an important accent, further enhancing this "living room" that just happens to be a bath.

Opposite: *Richly embellished in every detail, this lavish bath features some show-stopping elements, notably the soaking tub surrounded in marble and the unique multidimensional ceiling in warm gold and black.* Architect: Charles Cunniffe Architects.

Ceramic tile has been admired for its durable, brilliant color and shine since the earliest civilizations. This bath pays willing homage to the beauty of tile with a design that evokes all the romance of ancient and medieval days. Alluding to the cultures of Byzantium and Moorish Spain, among others, the space features a spirited mix of small glossy blue and green tiles; medium-size tiles in an ombré range of burnt umber, tan, and other earthy tones; and large tiles in pale, neutral tones embellished with intricate traditional motifs you'd expect to see on a shrine. The combination sounds challenging, but the visual effect is layered, rich, and dazzling in a surprisingly subtle way. The romantic at heart might say that the effect is one of happening across an archeological find of some sort. While it's not Pompeii, it's certainly a treasure trove of timeless design ideas.

Opposite: *A bather in this unique space enters another world. A sunken tub lined in small stone blue tiles and surrounded by larger tiles in warm-hued umber gives the slightly mysterious feeling of a pool in an ancient grotto. Arched windows let in ample light without compromising privacy and contribute to the ancient, romantic feeling.*
Designer: Rogers-Ford, L.C. Stone: Walker Zanger.

A glass door with a scrolled brass handle and arched, open top beckons into the private enclave of the sunken tub area. The arch motif is repeated in the row of small, beautifully proportioned windows in the tub area.

Above: *Pretty primroses in botanically correct hues accent the beige tiles around the tub as well as the crisp white wallcovering. White wood shutters preserve privacy with tradition; a charming antique ice cream parlor chair in durable wire keeps towels handy.*

Lots of bright white enlivened by rosy red and other garden colors give this Victorian-inspired bath a cheerful feeling that makes getting ready in the morning a pleasure. This room is spacious, but the design techniques used would be just as attractive in a smaller space. White-painted cabinetry spans one whole wall to give this master bath an enviable amount of storage without being visually oppressive. A vanity runs almost the entire length of the opposite wall, giving each user plenty of elbowroom at the sink as well as offering space for a makeup table in between. Above the vanity, a large frameless mirror with beveled edges is topped by theatrical lighting and is positioned to capture even more light from the pair of large windows above the tub. A private toilet compartment, decorated as nicely as the rest of the bath, is an extra-thoughtful touch in a room filled with creature comforts.

Left: *Marble tile in a mottled beige offers a subtle variation on all the bright white cabinetry. Tiles used on the vanity countertop are smaller than those on the floor to preserve pleasing proportions; dark-toned grout minimizes upkeep.*

Opposite: *A pair of doors with a transom window leads into this bright bath enriched with cottage charm. A flowery rug would be expected, but this red, white, blue, and gray rug in a surprising Native American–inspired design sets the cheerful color scheme without being predictable. Botanical wallcovering filled with rows of multicolored primroses adds a sprightly garden prettiness.*

Silvery tones on the mirror and the tub's claw feet look great with classic chrome tub fittings. Their cool sparkle looks especially fresh in contrast to the unpolished wood floor and the mottled, antique-look tub and blanket stand-turned-towel rack.

Fʀᴏᴍ Cᴀɴᴛᴏɴ to Copenhagen, white cut with blue (especially intense, midtone cobalt or royal blue) has won hearts through the ages. These two baths take this perennially popular pairing to regal new heights with the addition of gold and silver accents. In one room, golden embellishments make the tub into an eye-catching, formal focal point. In the other, an artfully crafted round mirror with a hammered-silver frame makes a celestial statement that is echoed by subtle silvery tones in an otherwise-rustic space. Both rooms are swathed in rich blue backgrounds that make neutrals—from the plain wood floors to the metallic accents—really shine. If blue's not for you, try this treatment with another color. This concept would have an entirely different look—and feeling—with walls of, for example, raspberry, lime, or evergreen, but the result would be the same: sophisticated, confident, and luscious!

Opposite: *An ornately embellished tub gleams with the beautiful combination of royal blue and brilliant gold. Cut with lots of sparkling white, the look is cheerful and romantic. Gilt touches in the mirror and fittings carry the confident theme.*

A GENEROUSLY SCALED BATH can be luxurious without being overly formal, as this welcoming space proves. One friendly element is the wonderful quality of the light. Custom windows with genuine divided mullions are undeniably elegant, but their main purpose here is to flood the room with natural sunshine and give the owners a liberating view outdoors. Another inviting element is the use of warm-hued mosaic tiles throughout the room. The patterns are lively but somehow timeless, recalling ethnic weavings or patchwork quilts. Whatever the origins they evoke, the colored tiles add visual interest and warmth underscored by touches of rustic wood and stone. Items in warm, textured wood, such as a lightly scaled vanity chair, a mirror, and candlesticks, are important contrasts to the cool surfaces of tile, porcelain, and stone that predominate in any bath. The fireplace just outside the clear glass shower stall is an unusual indulgence, but it's perfectly at home in a bath that's all about low-key luxury.

Above: *The clear shower surround offers an unobstructed view of yet another mosaic tile design. A similar tile treatment on the fireplace surround adds visual warmth and interest and creates a dramatic focal point.*

Opposite: *Mosaic tiles in a timeless pattern suggest ethnic weavings, patchwork quilts, and other comforting images. Over the tub, they form a handsome focal point that withstands splashes better than framed art.*

Left: *A two-level vanity counter in richly patterned marble is beautiful and practical. A huge Palladian-style window opens the space to the view and an abundance of natural light, a great luxury in any bath.*

Love Affair With Color

CHOOSING FABRIC in the colors you love is a foolproof way to start a decorating scheme. These homeowners selected the energizing combination of scarlet red, golden yellow, and bright white to wake up a their bath. The scheme is never oppressive, thanks to a fairly spacious floor plan and lots of white, including all the fixtures and an unusual floor that looks like paper lace. The room also owes its charm to the softening influence of pretty, traditional touches, artfully repeated in varying ways. A scalloped line, for example, appears in the sink's classic rope detailing and shell-shape bowl, the antique screen, the Austrian balloon shade, and even on the edge of the red towels. Touches of black ground those hot colors and add a sophisticated finish to the setting. If your bath is older and you don't want to change the wall tiles or pull out the built-in tub, see how much difference a new sink, toilet, and color scheme can make!

Opposite: *Traditional style is no stranger to strong colors, but today's take is brighter and more sophisticated, as seen here. This Victorian-inspired bath takes a couple of passionate colors and sets them off with lots of white and a bit of black. A modern toilet is the only contemporary fixture here, but the overall look is fresh.*

Left: *A virtuoso pedestal sink with rope detailing and fittings in antiqued brass and porcelain looks wonderful beneath a mahogany mirror embellished with gilded motifs and faux tassels in red and gold. A narrow wallpaper border in white and gold bridges the painted and tiled sections of the wall.*

Above: *This bath owes a lot to its spectacular view, but even without the Colorado mountains, the space would be impressive. Grandly scaled, it has a livable ambience because it relies more on fine materials than complicated details. A case in point: the excitingly patterned marble tub surround and shower stall.* Architect: Charles Cunniffe Architects. **Opposite:** *The focal point of the room, a picture window that spans almost the entire length of the oval tub, is framed by marble tiles and visually anchored by the marble-surround tub. A divided-lite window would be more conventionally traditional, but an austerely simple sheet of glass lets the view— and the patterned marble—star.*

WHILE THERE'S NO SUBSTITUTE for a wonderful scenic view, you can create interior vistas worth looking at with some of nature's most spectacular materials: granite and marble. In both of these master baths, marble with exciting high-contrast veining captures the lion's share of attention indoors, which is just what the owners wanted. Although these baths also feature high ceilings, generous square footage, nicely crafted wood cabinets, and yes, great views, it's the marble in the tub and shower areas that makes the rooms so distinctive. In one bath, the palette is carried through with plush wall-to-wall carpeting in the same tones as the marble; in the other, stone tiles punctuated with black tile diamonds make a classic statement. Natural stone comes in a variety of colors, and natural veining adds even more variation, so you're sure to find stone that enhances whatever color scheme you're planning. Stone tiles are more affordable than slabs, too.

WHITE HAS BEEN a popular bath color ever since indoor plumbing transformed our lives, but the power of white goes beyond the safe choice of white porcelain fixtures. The walls of these two traditional-style baths are swathed in the pearly hue for a romantic and spacious effect. Against them, white fixtures create an interesting white-on-white tonal pattern. To keep the whole effect from visually floating away, both baths are safely grounded with darker tones of terra-cotta tile and wood. Neither of these materials is typical for bath floors, but they give the all-white rooms a more substantial, timeless feeling. In another unusual move, the exteriors of both tubs are painted in pale tints the color of Wedgwood Jasperware: one light blue, the other light green. These tints, a pretty bridge between dark floors and soaring white walls, give the baths a novel touch that is unquestionably charming.

A white sink as decorative as a wedding cake makes a fun, pretty focal point for this unashamedly romantic bath. The vintage-style two-piece toilet and claw-foot tub further the decorative Victorian ambience.

Opposite: *Matte terra-cotta tiles are an unusual flooring material for a pretty, traditional-style bath, but in this case, the tiles serve to ground the predominantly white room. Pale celadon green on the border tiles and matching claw-foot tub makes a pleasing transition between floor and walls.*

BLUE AND WHITE, one of the best-loved color schemes for bedrooms and baths, can take on a wide variety of looks, depending on other elements in the space. In one bath shown here, an abundance of strongly grained oak wood lends a down-to-earth warmth to the space, while blue functions as a minor accent color. In the other, blue combines with an array of unabashedly romantic elements—lace, dried rosebuds, and ruffled fabrics—to create a fun, frivolous air. The different feeling of these two rooms is the result of many savvy decorating choices. For example, tailored, checked café curtains provide a much different effect than a silky, ruffled Austrian shade; vintage stoneware makes a different statement than porcelain. To keep the schemes from looking too predictable, the designers added a frilly wallcovering border into the tailored room and a homespun rag rug into the pretty one. Even a classic color scheme can use a surprise or two!

Right: *A periwinkle blue Austrian shade adds a lavish touch to this romantic country bath inspired by all things Victorian. The antique pedestal sink joins other charming old bathing accoutrements; beyond, a modern combination shower/tub with its ribbons-and-roses curtain offers more up-to-date convenience.*

Opposite: *A fortunate woman in the Old West would surely cozy up to this blue, white, and oak bath, where rustic good looks and nostalgic charm live happily together. The golden brown tones of the wood are a beautiful contrast to the cool tones of the blue-and-white stoneware collection, some of it antique.*

Neutral Territory

Along, RELATIVELY NARROW BATH packs in all the luxuries in style, thanks to a space-expanding neutral color scheme and savvy engineering. Each function has its own space: At one end of the bath there's a private compartment for the bidet and toilet; the other end offers a soaking tub. One long wall holds the shower stall; the other, two spacious vanity cabinets. Luxurious materials used with restraint have a lot to do with this bathroom's clean-cut yet traditional elegance. Below the chair-rail level, beige marble tiles cover the walls and extend onto the floor. Above, a subtly striped ivory-and-beige wallcovering echoes the natural striations in the marble. To keep things from looking too bland or pale, vanity cabinets, a Chinese box-shape basket, a cabriole-leg stool, and an antique-look runner rug—all in rich tones of brown—add warmth and contrast without closing up the space.

Left: *Artfully curved marble backsplash sides give these marble vanity tops extra architectural cachet. Dark, finely grained wood cabinets and a subtle tone-on-tone striped wallcovering are classically elegant. A three-shelf open cabinet built into a wall offers extra storage without intruding on the space, and a skylight flanked by recessed ceiling fixtures provides good visibility 'round the clock.*

Opposite: *A roomy soaking tub enclosed in marble tiles becomes a special focal point thanks to a dramatically arched ceiling over the tub alcove. A carefully selected array of dark-toned antiques relieves the monochromatic scheme and adds important elegant accents. Tall casement windows covered in shirred neutral-print fabrics are pretty but not too sweet.*

THE LOOK OF A LODGE or cabin is particularly popular now, but its natural appeal is truly timeless. Both of these bathrooms use the lodge look to create the feeling of a getaway retreat, so it's no wonder that both position the soaking tubs beneath large windows that suggest panoramic views. One bath features a generously sized double vanity; in the other, the vanities are separate. But each solution gives a couple plenty of room— a necessary recipe for stress reduction. Lots of natural-finished wood defines the lodge look, while pretty touches keep it from becoming too much of a good thing. In one bath, Victorian-style glass lamp globes and blush-toned tile offer charming contrast; the other uses ruffled, plaid lampshades and a colorfully patterned rug to perform the same task in a slightly more tailored way. In both, traditional floral-sprigged wallcoverings add a sentimental flourish to baths that epitomize hearty, no-nonsense style.

A vaulted ceiling, curved windows over the tub alcove, and unusual peeled log facings create a dramatic effect that's both rustic and architecturally sophisticated. Even the drawer handles are made of varnished branches.

Opposite: *Heavy, full-round log beams span the length of the ceiling for a rustic look that contrasts interestingly with the refined marble tile floor and tub surround. Hunter green ceramic tiles and natural-stained oak cabinets further the woodsy palette.*

Castle Keep

THE DANCING PRINCESSES from the French fairy tale would be perfectly at home in this exquisite bath. Romantic, *mais oui,* but if you covet this look, you'll find many of its elements in historical architectural drawings. A multitude of fine details build up an ambience that recalls the light-hearted elegance of 17th- and 18th-century *chateaux.* Rendered entirely in tender tones of oyster white and pale taupe, the room has a mellow, antique air without sacrificing one whit of cleanliness or modern convenience. The woodwork is beautifully balanced, with cabinet doors that take their lines from heavy castle doors and drawers that are embellished with faux-stone quoins, the stacked blocks of exposed stone around many European doorways. The room's doorways are millwork masterpieces, beautifully curved and set in handsome columns. Above, large mirrors framed in delicate carving are lit by perfectly scaled candelabra sconces. No detail is overlooked or overdone. But how very French, *n'est-ce pas?*

Left: *Exquisite woodwork distinguishes this elegant fairy-tale bath. Built-in mirrors framed by curved, scroll-embellished wood are a classic French treatment that really comes into its own here. The gently curved corner cabinet units are accented by faux-stone quoins, yet another French icon.*

Opposite: *Antique white tones that evoke French limestone and beautifully carved woodwork convey a timeless, subtle opulence. The single vanity sink leaves plenty of counterspace for beauty aids and favorite accessories.* Designer: Randy Sisk, Kitchens by Kleweno. Cabinets: Draper-DBS, Inc.

A PREDOMINANTLY WHITE BATH has universal appeal, but there are as many moods to white as there are people to appreciate them. In this king-size master bath, an air of well-bred, quiet luxury has been established through an array of deftly understated touches. Most of these make use of white on white—a scheme that seems to render even the most whimsical elements witty rather than cutesy. The result is a layered, rich look that exudes dignity and gives one a sense of the owners' personalities, too. The teak and white wood tub surround, for example, evokes both classic architecture and the timeless appeal of ships. The vanity cabinets, traditionally simple except for exotic touches of bamboo trim, recall tropical English plantation influences. The shower stall is a masterpiece of white-on-white tiles in classic rope and marine-life motifs. The overall effect of these signature elements is seaworthy but not clichéd.

Above: *A shower lined in antique-looking tiles is even more beguiling thanks to dimensional accent tiles depicting shells, sand dollars, and starfish. Unlacquered brass fittings and a built-in seat of softly mottled polished stone enhance the underwater mystique.*

Right: *Custom-made cabinets are trimmed in bamboo for a subtly exotic touch. The ivory wallcovering and coordinating oyster white tile vanity trim are beautifully textured for a quiet opulence. The plantation look is enhanced by the door's fixed-louver top that lets air circulate but protects privacy.*

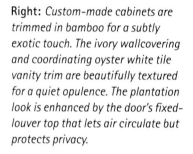

Opposite: *A state-of-the-art tub is enriched with a teak deck protected by a fiberglass finish and a traditional recessed-panel surround. The tub is positioned to allow bathers to enjoy a seaside view.* Designer: Andrea LeShay, Design for Sale. Architect: Peter Cook, AIA. Fittings: Newport Brass.

Above: *If you have the space, take a tip from this elegant room and include "real" furniture like this round white end table and mahogany-finished side chair. Extra places to set toiletries are always appreciated, as is a comfy place to sit. The pediment-top vanity cabinet continues the freestanding furniture look.*

You don't need acres of marble to create a luxurious bathroom. In this deceptively simple space, neoclassical and Renaissance elements blend with consummate grace to create a lovely bath. Its restrained palette offers both warmth and elegance: The room is wrapped in a peach-gold with the look of aged Italian frescoes, freshened with verdigris green, and accented with the exciting contrast of ivory and ebony. In homage to the room's inspiration as well as the basics of fine interior design, nothing is overdone and every detail is in harmony with the color scheme and the neoclassical and Renaissance theme. Even the drapery, with its laurel wreath motif, harkens back to the ancient Greece from which the Renaissance gained so much. The pediment-top vanity offers the popular look of freestanding furniture and creates an impressive yet restrained focal point, and the black-and-white marble floor tiles are formal and timeless.

Left: *Discreetly tucked into an alcove created by the shower stall, the bidet, a warming towel rack, and a vintage-style toilet are out of the way but accessible. Architectural drawings carry the room's neoclassical theme.*

Right: *Rich tones of Renaissance oil paintings are echoed in the tawny hues of the walls, while ancient architectural drawings offer crisp black-and-white accents. A claw-foot tub, boldly painted black, is a focal point that works surprisingly well with the delicately tinted, gracefully scaled tables nearby.*

FLOWER GARDENS FLOURISH in the cool, damp weather of England, so even when skies are gray, the fields are a riot of soft colors. Some of the world's most beautiful floral wallcoverings and fabrics celebrate this lovely phenomenon, and there's no easier way to evoke English country style than with an array of flower patterns. To keep the look from becoming distractingly cluttered in a small bath, choose a color palette—here, it's green, rose, and white—and play it out in different tones and proportions throughout the room. In one bath, a predominantly white ground supports a wide range of patterns-on-patterns; in the other, a stronger green-and-white scheme relies on flower motifs in lacy patterns as well as in colorful prints. Small formal rugs and accent furniture in cherry, mahogany, and bamboo add a Victorian touch that is irresistibly romantic and cozy.

Opposite: *Layers of delicate floral and vine patterns make this small bath a winsome one. In true English country style, the patterns aren't matched, but with their predominantly pink flowers and soothing white or soft green grounds, they all work prettily together.*

A color scheme of hunter green and crisp white gives this vintage-style bath a rich look. The lacy window curtains and romantic cutwork shower curtain set off the Art Nouveau–inspired tub decoration and brighten the room's deep-tone walls.

A spectacular vanity cabinet with superbly matched wood grains and intricate ebonized detailing and hardware lends an exotic air to this bath. The mirrored wall, hung with gleaming chandelier sconces, enhances the elegant excitement of this space. Designer: Betsy Meyer, CKD, CBD, Betsy Meyer Associates, Inc. Interior Designer: Jeanne Leonard, Jeanne Leonard Interiors, Inc.

Viewers of this spacious master bath might have a bit of difficulty singling out just one focal point. The spectacular vanity with its pair of crystal sconces is certainly a show-stopper. But the marble-surrounded tub with its window view flanked by classic oval windows is also unquestionably eye-catching. Even if your bath isn't large enough to have more than one focal point, you can still take a few tips from this handsome room. Position a large mirror opposite the window if possible to capture all the light as well as the view, if it's a pleasing one. (If it's not, a pretty translucent shade or curtain that obscures the scene but admits the light will do.) Install vanity lighting right on or above the mirror for more reflective sparkle. For the crowning touch, find a vintage dresser and have it converted into a unique vanity, or just embellish an ordinary vanity with special paint and hardware.

Deceptively simple, this tub surround in fine wood gains added richness from the swirling grained marble top that extends onto adjacent walls. Extending the surround onto nearby walls is clever in several ways: It gives the whole room a sleek, flowing look and provides ample space for both seating and stacking bath supplies.

A freestanding claw-foot tub rests on a slab of genuine marble—a clever way to protect the wall-to-wall carpeting from excess moisture without disturbing the luxe scheme of the space. A massive vanity and golden toile de Jouy wallcovering further the 18th-century look but in pale tones to preserve the room's spaciousness.

Large or small, just about any bath can be made to look lavish with the careful layering of luxurious little touches everywhere. In the smaller bath here, the color scheme—a refined mix of plum, sage, and antique ivory—is romantic yet dignified. A handsome shower curtain with coordinating damask-look fabrics on each side makes an unexpected but impressive focal point. A coordinating smocked valance, trimmed in tawny chenille, is a look you'd expect on a costly upholstered piece. Here, it lends special importance to the whole room as it frames the tub and offers a measure of privacy to the toilet area. In the larger bath, swagged-and-bowed curtains and a chandelier you'd expect to see in a formal dining room make an enchanting impression. In both, graceful gilt-framed oval mirrors, large-scale floral arrangements (in neutral tones so as not to overwhelm), and other charming touches give the look of country manor living rooms.

Below left: *An obvious focal point of this appealing bath is the opulent shower curtain. Using two coordinating fabrics with an elegant damask look, this curtain is as beautiful on the inside as it is on the outside. The freestanding furniture vanity outfitted with a pretty drop-in sink sports another traditional living room icon: a heavy tassel.* Designer: Bacarella Martin Interiors. **Below right:** *Golden tones in the subtle wallcovering and pine wood vanity "read" quietly neutral yet also reference the golden tones in the damask fabric, brass accessories, and gilt-framed mirror. Rather than filling up the space with a welter of countrified knickknacks, this design uses a carefully edited collection of special accessories—and that makes all the difference.*

A BATH THAT'S BIGGER than most bedrooms deserves a larger-than-life design concept, and that's just what the designer gave this intriguing beauty. A sleek, footed tub makes a handsome centerpiece to the room, but it's the wonderfully frivolous window treatment—white sheers treated like damask draperies—and the fireplace that really captivate. The fireplace, a working model, gains even more importance from its pretty, carved 18th-century mantel. Moldings from the same era style embellish the perimeter of the room and the fronts of the separate but equal vanity cabinets. Dramatic touches, like the leopard painting over the mantel and the line-and-wash drawings above the bidet area, delight in the unexpected. In detail after detail, the design sets a tone that hints this room is a bit more adventurous than other elegant, traditional rooms. And isn't that bit of unexpected adventure what romance is all about?

Left: *A streamlined version of the vintage claw-foot tub has all the charm of the original but with architectural flair. The angled, marble shower stall and the towel warmer behind the bidet are luxuries perfectly suited to this regal space.*

Opposite: *Translucent drifts of snowy, billowing window sheers swathe this bathroom's exceptionally large window in romance. A working fireplace with an ornate 18th-century mantel gets an extra jolt of drama from an enigmatic portrait of a leopard.*

Every bath can do with a grand gesture that lifts it out of the ordinary. In some, it may be an adventurous color scheme or a remarkable surfacing material; in others, it's a wonderful architectural detail. This spacious bath belongs in the last category: Its big, beautiful window at the foot of the tub recalls the Palladian windows in the foyers of grand country homes. Following the architecturally inspired theme, the tub also borrows from the elegant past with classical molding along its visible side. While you may not be able to fit in the window, the tub molding, easily found at builder's supply and craft stores, would enrich any traditional-style bath. An abundance of white marble on the floors and walls makes a fabulous impression while preserving the clean, open aesthetic of the room. Against this pale, luxurious background, ornately carved, dark mahogany furniture pieces look especially dramatic and beautiful.

White marble and lots of mirrors are a foolproof recipe for a luxurious bath. What makes this space even more special are the boudoir touches of "real" furniture in mahogany that provide storage next to the handsome pedestal sink.

Opposite: *A generously sized, gracefully arched window at the foot of the tub gives this bath a king-size dose of what may be the ultimate luxury: lots of natural light. The British Colonial étagère and stool add a touch of the exotic.*

Filled with beguiling details, this powder room looks like it's straight out of a French fairy tale from the 1700s. The gilded wood mirror frame with its faux drapery is echoed in the faux-painted drapery above the door. A hand-painted sink adds panache. Designer: Mary T. Liebhold, CKD, The Kitchen Specialist, Inc. Cabinets: Heritage Custom Kitchens.

THERE'S NO MISTAKING the French influence in these baths. Refined but not stuffy, they're filled with élan and a quintessentially chic spirit. One, enlisting the spirit of Cinderella or perhaps Marie Antoinette, has a distinctly coquettish air. Faux accents are at their finest here, such as the painted drapery rod and swathe over the door that complements the faux drapery on the vanity mirror. The other bath, a restrained homage to the Napoleonic Empire period, uses black accents to create excitement with elegance. (The old designer's dictum that every room can benefit from a bit of shiny black gets put to good use in these two rooms.) What's key to keeping these decorating ideas from becoming clichéd? Sophisticated, largely neutral color schemes confined to a palette of white, cream, tan, brown, and black, plus a wash of sage green in one and a hint of old rose in the other.

Opposite: *Like its inspiration, Napoleon, this Empire-style bath makes up for its small size with a big vision and a confident air. A black metal side table with characteristic Empire crossed-lance legs offers space for a few extra toiletries and accessories.* Designer: Jere Bowden, CKD, Rutt of Atlanta. Interior designer: Jay Miner, Miner Details. Manufacturer: Rutt of Atlanta.

As ageless as the logs from which they're made, these baths celebrate the timeless, soothing appeal of America's great forests. In keeping with the spirit of these rooms, virtually every surface is a top-quality natural material designed to last for many generations. One bath uses marble for both the floor and vanity countertop; the other uses mottled granite for the countertop and boasts a window adorned with delicate wood fretwork. Both have a combination of half-round logs and planed boards that create interest and variety while using woods in the same honey tones. Another classic material, albeit synthetic, is the white porcelain used for sinks. The drop-in model appears somewhat more nostalgic, while the undermount version is rather contemporary, but both offer low-maintenance good looks that will stand the test of time. Touches of black in hardware and accessories evoke the rustic wrought iron of olden days and add a dash of contrast.

One of the baths in the honeymoon cabin at Cape Topridge, the former Adirondack retreat of heiress Marjorie Meriwether Post, this setting would be romantic anywhere. Diamond-shape divided lites in the casement windows are echoed in the vanity light fixture. Designer: Rogers-Ford, L.C. Architect: Michael Bird, Adirondack Design Associates.

Right: *Chic black sconces and mini hanging lamps give this golden-hued bath the needed zip of contrast. In homage to natural tones and materials, the salmon brown genuine marble countertops and mottled tan marble tile floor blend smoothly in with the wood cabinets and log walls.* Builder: Rocky Mountain Log Homes.

UNABASHED ROMANTICISM reigns in both of these very different baths. What they have in common is a basic placement of fixtures, a penchant for the grand gesture, and a preference for flattering makeup colors such as pink, mauve, and peach anchored by sophisticated taupe and rich brown neutrals. Beyond that, these two rooms show how differently romantic style can be interpreted to suit personal tastes. In one, a refined opulence is achieved with peach silk on the windows, peach marble on the floor, and a lovely substantial vanity and mirror embellished with faux finishing in subtle peach-and-taupe tones. In the other, pink plumes and pretty touches make for an irrepressible send-up of Victorian style. Whatever "romantic" style means to you, you can create it even in the smallest space. Don't be afraid of an over-the-top idea, either very dramatic or sweetly whimsical: Both moods make for a room that goes beyond the everyday. And that's the essence of romantic style.

Simply "mauve-lous," this whimsical, Victorian-inspired powder room makes a strong decorating statement in a tiny space. A spectacular antique dresser crafted of natural tiger-striped wood and topped with a curvaceous mirror makes a unique vanity.

Opposite: Awash in flattering peach and taupe tones, this traditionally elegant guest bath features peach marble floors with coordinating faux-finished cabinets. The window is covered with pleated sheers and peach silk balloon shades. Designer: John Robert Wiltgen, John Robert Wiltgen Designs, Inc.

WHILE IT'S EASY to add glitz and glamour to a space, there are a few timeless indicators of quality that can't be faked. In architecture and design, one such indicator is the luxury of space, which this room shares with many other baths in luxury homes today. The other indicator is the masterful execution of brilliant designs—a quality that's much rarer. Happily, this room has that quality in abundance. The result is a room that is graceful, intelligent, beautifully simple, and excitingly opulent, all at the same time. This master bath is animated by a confident interpretation of neoclassical style, carefully executed. While the layout is simple, each element is a masterpiece of its kind. The genuine marble floor is incised with a starburst design, the tub is paneled with classical mouldings, and the vanity is meticulously fitted with mirrors. Any one of these would be eye-catching, but all of them together add up to one simply spectacular setting.

Right: *Slightly curved to follow the rounded lines of the room's wall, this deftly engineered vanity gets a surprisingly dramatic touch with a front that's set with precisely cut mirrors. Crystal cabinet knobs and discreetly scaled sconces mounted on the mirror above enhance the sparkling look.*

Opposite: *A wonderful starburst pattern created by marble of contrasting colors bespeaks a timeless refinement and opulence in this rotunda-shape bath. A tub embellished with classical paneling and centered on the starburst adds even more drama.*

Below: *Warm golden tones refreshed by sharp black and white give this Empire-inspired bath a great dignity and vigor that would make any owner feel like a prince of the realm. Slender columns set off the bathtub alcove, one of this bath's many clever allusions to classicism.*

Tʜᴇꜱᴇ ʙᴀᴛʜꜱ, while equipped with modern conveniences we've come to depend on, clearly hearken back to the elegant, many-layered past. In one, a black-and-white-and-gold scheme recalls the Empire period of Napoleon, which itself borrowed images and motifs from another empire: ancient Rome. In this space, the use of a columnar pedestal sink and architectural fragments as accessories is very apt. A later but no less august empire, that of England in the era of Queen Victoria, is evoked in the other bath, again with some artful French and Mediterranean influences. In this room, a warm taupe for the toilet and sink lends a soft, antiqued look, augmented by the rustic, overscale gray and terra-cotta tiles. In both these baths, neutral colors show how rich and eloquent they can be. Light-capturing white and special touches, like the artworks matted in gold, add to the quietly opulent mood.

Opposite: *Romantic yet elegant, this bath evokes the spirit of a 19th-century European room without sacrificing any creature comforts. A Giacometti-inspired ceiling lamp, upholstered bergere chair, and small gilded table create a room for living, not just bathing. A simply curtained claw-foot tub and a generously scaled sink are luxurious basics.*

CONTEMPORARY STYLE embraces a fairly wide range of looks. "Modern" design is officially pegged to begin with the Arts & Crafts/Mission styles that arose in the early 20th century as a revolt against the fussiness of Victorian traditional style, but in the early 21st century, "modern" is popularly used to describe design icons from the 1930s to the '60s. "Contemporary," sometimes used interchangeably with the word "modern," is less a structured concept and more a way of life.

Contemporary is cool and clean and can be as casual or as elegant as you please. Because so much of a bath is dominated by modern fixtures anyway, many people simply choose contemporary style, regardless of what they're using in the rest of the house. In general, contemporary style appears simpler than traditional: Curves are looser and more sculptural; squared-off angles are commonplace; surface details are minimized or eliminated; and textures, rather than representational images, offer interest. Sculptural one-piece toilets, sleek built-ins of all kinds, minimal or simply shaped hardware, and lots of chrome are all contemporary design elements. Some modern-style products make a point of revealing their structure and function where traditional style would take pains to disguise them. Others reduce forms to their simplest, essential expression, easily seen in abstract patterns of dolphins, leaves, etc., in contemporary fabric designs. Contemporary style is easily at home in the modern bath, since it's of the same generation. Whether the look is dramatic or serene, contemporary style at its best conveys an uplifting spirit of freshness and freedom.

CALIFORNIA SPA

At home in transitional settings, this most popular of contemporary styles is softer than modern, cleaner than traditional, and easy to live with. Often credited to the legendary late designer Michael Taylor, refreshing yet sophisticated California style uses the neutrals of baskets, sea sponges, and driftwood plus every tone of white-on-white, from warm ivory to cool oyster-shell gray. Soft pastels the color of sea glass may also play a part: Celadon (pale gray-green), lettuce (light yellow-green), and periwinkle (pastel blue-violet) are current favorites. Look for overscaled, sleekly styled white porcelain spa tubs, pedestal sinks, or drop-in sinks in bleached-wood vanity cabinets. Your cabinets may be frameless and hardware free; adorned with modern hardware in a silvery, brushed-nickel finish; or embellished with arty, offbeat hardware, such as pewter starfish. Floors may be anything pale, beautiful, and practical: white marble (real or faux) or oversize white ceramic tiles laid on the diagonal to maximize space. Fluffy towels in white, sand, and ecru, and a few big shells to hold soaps are all the accessories you need.

SCANDINAVIAN

Scandinavian contemporary, a less serious cousin of the 1950's Scandinavian modern, is a cheerful look that pairs whites and light wood tones with one or more bright primary colors. It's a can't-miss look for a kid's bath or one with a snappy sailing theme. A vanity painted glossy white is a fresh look; naturally finished pale woods such as ash and beech make a nice alternative. A white porcelain drop-in sink has a simple, clean look; add a goose-neck faucet and fittings in colorful enameled steel

for a jolt of fun and fashion. For an interesting alternative to red/yellow/blue with white, choose intense secondary and tertiary colors such as teal, violet, and yellow-orange or lime. For long-term versatility, confine strong colors to towels and accessories, or choose the most staid of them—royal blue and teal are bath favorites that work with many other colors—for your border tiles and other installed accents.

Art Deco

This frankly glamorous style from the 1920s and '30s is well-suited to a contemporary bath where an extra bit of cool and drama is required. Based on white, ivory, and gray plus black and cool metallic tones, Art Deco is sophisticated and sleek. If you'd like a bit more color, add tropical aqua and coral for a Miami influence, ice blue and mauve for the New York-to-Paris variant. Stylized, leaping antelopes,

Lots of brilliant white and softly polished, natural-hued wood create a lovely, spacious ambience in this bath inspired by California spa designs. Fixtures and fittings: American Standard.

lotus flowers, palmetto leaves, and other exotic images of nature bring the Art Deco look to your ceramic tile borders and wallcoverings. Traditional white pedestal sinks à la Grand Hotel and gleaming chrome fittings are perfect for this look, along with lots of mirrors. For accessories, look for silvery mercury glass and frosted glass. If you prefer a vanity sink, look for one in blonde wood with chrome banding and hardware, or have a vintage "moderne" chest of drawers converted. A pale marble, solid-surfacing, or laminate vanity countertop is a natural. Because it's a historical style, although a relatively recent one, Art Deco can be used to good effect in a traditional home. In fact, if you live in a pre-WWII-era house, you may find that a lot of existing elements, such as tile, are already in place in your bath!

Urban Loft

This savvy style owes its flair to Milan-style modern and its grit to industrial chic. Simple shapes in remarkable materials are key to the look; for example, see how polished granite, art glass, and stainless steel add light-catching sparkle to the space. Choose a streamlined pedestal sink or a vanity with an interesting sink—perhaps hammered stainless steel or an art-glass bowl that sits entirely on top of the counter. For the vanity, choose a frameless, solid hardwood or metal model with finger grooves or modern statement-making door and drawer pulls. (For a slightly funkier 1950's brand of modern, spark the look with chrome banding, edges, and hardware, but skip the grooved designs—they're hard to clean). For the countertop, choose the smooth sweep of marble or granite (black with mica

An antique tub in a modern industrial loft space strikes a witty note in this simple, sophisticated bath. An ample array of hooks offers easily accessible storage. Designer: Sallie Trout, Trout Studios.

Imaginative and original, this urbane bath evokes the glitter of city lights at night with its glass-tiled wall and sparkling metallic accents. Designer: James R. Dase, CKD, CBD, Kohler. Tile: Ann Sacks Tile & Stone.

tiles or high-gloss paint in white or, if space allows, a dramatic color that's decoratively inset in a backsplash. For accent colors, repeat your dramatic color, and add a few others—acid green, teal or violet-blue, lush cantaloupe or scarlet—and carry it out in accessories sparked with chrome and black.

RETRO

Fun, funky, and confident, retro modern celebrates that bright, brash look from the 1940s and '50s. This practical style is great for a kid's bath or one off the family rec room: It offers easy cleaning with lots of glossy surfaces plus a look that's young, cheerful, and energetic. To start, take your basic white bath, toss in a few bright primary colors and hot pastels (perhaps red, turquoise, and yellow, or coral, mint, and royal blue), and mix in a pinch or two of black for drama. The classic retro look is a white pedestal sink; if you need the room, try a wood vanity painted in high-gloss white or, for the adventurous, metal finished with appliance-grade paints. Accent with shiny modern chrome fittings, and scour flea markets and architectural salvage dealers for chrome counter edging, fittings, and vintage modern cabinet hardware. Choose retro-patterned vinyl or linoleum flooring and laminate countertops. Finish it off with perky café curtains or a valance in retro-print fabrics (available new or in savvy flea market shops) over metal Venetian blinds, with a matching shower curtain. For accessories, choose any memorabilia that has a practical use, such as cartoon character mugs as toothbrush holders. With a slight shift of colors (lime instead of mint, for example) plus different fabric and laminate patterns, your retro look could flash forward to the early '60s.

chips is dynamite) or plain solid surfacing, perhaps in gunmetal gray. If your budget decrees laminates, go either very plain or with a funky, abstract pattern or texture, and don't be afraid of showing a lot of metal, especially chrome and stainless steel. Specify nonslip ceramic, natural stone, or even commercial rubber floor tiles. For your shower curtain, choose an abstract print in adventurous color combinations or in neutrals with an interesting texture. Window treatments should be minimal: Here's the place for narrow metal miniblinds or a Roman shade in cotton duck. Go for glossy ceramic wall

WHAT MAKES a contemporary design qualify as "romantic?" A look at this bath yields some clues. Perhaps it's the dramatically grained oak of the cabinets and vanity, stained so that the grain is even more pronounced. Maybe it's the unabashedly tender (yet amusingly retro) tones of the pink and green stained glass in the door. Or maybe it's the scattered leaves applied with careful randomness to the wall. Most likely, it's a combination of all these elements and more, all carefully orchestrated. For example, the pink glass of the door is repeated in the gerbera daisies on the vanity (in a green glass vase, of course) and in the pink glass of the Art Deco–inspired light fixture just visible over the vanity. In this tactic, the owner successfully follows the classic design rule of using a color at least three times within a setting—proof that even the most modern design can benefit from some traditional tips.

Right: *This wood cabinet's purpose is to provide as much bath storage as possible, but it also adds to the design excitement of the room. The choice of cabinet material, oak with a dramatically pronounced whorled grain, provides the important element of visual texture to this deceptively simple bath.*

Left: *A shower stall under the highest part of the roof shares a wall with a soaking tub positioned under the angled eave—a deft use of space to fit everything in, in style. Mirrored walls bounce light from the angled skylight, making the bath look even more spacious.*

I F YOU'RE IN THE MARKET for a really fabulous, totally modern bath, this one offers great inspiration. But it also exhibits the intelligent use of design concepts that can work just as well in a smaller room. For example, this bath is obviously large, but even a small space will look bigger if you keep the vanity, walls, and flooring in the same light tones and smooth textures. If marble or solid-surfacing materials are outside the realm of your budget, there are plenty of good-looking laminates in pale, creamy tones to choose from. Frameless mirrors are proven winners in creating a more spacious, brighter atmosphere; here, a row of mirrored medicine cabinets offers storage as well as dazzle. You may not have room for this many cabinets, but try a triptych (three-section) mirrored cabinet on one wall with the same model on the opposite or adjacent wall, and see how the space opens up.

Above: *You don't have to be a movie star or a sports star to enjoy the glamour of this spacious bath with all the comforts, and then some. A circular skylight echoes the line of the curved shower wall, balancing the array of square and rectangular volumes elsewhere in the space.*

A massive built-in marble vanity inset with a pair of squared-off sink bowls creates an austere and handsome design. The very modern horizontal line of the space is enhanced by the row of beveled-glass, mirrored vanity cabinets that hang above.

A built-in banquette seat, comfortably upholstered in moisture-resistant fabric the color of the walls, utilizes the classic roll pillows popular since ancient Roman times. Built-in lighted wall niches are architecturally striking as well as practical for storage and display. **Fixtures and fittings: Kohler.**

ENTERING THIS BATH is like stepping into an enchanted grotto or cavern. Tumbled marble tiles, slab marble tiles, and handmade tiles that look like elegant natural stone all pay tribute to the beauty of nature in this handsome bath. A mix of large, medium, and small tiles in a variety of hues and patterns swirls around the room, but the fantastic array of patterns and sizes is never dizzying thanks to the rich yet subdued range of earthy colors and patterns. To make a concept like this work takes careful planning of every detail and meticulous placement of every tile. That kind of artistry and care is clearly in evidence, even in small details. For example, to keep the room human-scaled, small diamond-shape tiles are set in channel-bordered rows at chair-rail height and above. Small, gleaming metallic tiles add jewel-like accents to this already beautiful space.

Above: *A vanity niche, mirrored on all sides, reflects the sparkle of a stainless-steel sink and the muted glow of brushed-nickel fittings. A slab of granite with a beveled edge tops a frameless vanity cabinet in beautifully grained hardwood. The wood bears an intriguing carved design echoed in the wardrobe doors.*

Opposite: *A shower stall with a frameless glass door lets the spectacular beauty of the stall's stone tiles show through. The visual drama inherent in these excitingly patterned tiles is enhanced by using different sizes of tiles and by setting some on the square, some on the diagonal.* Designer: Gene Pindzia, Riverside Custom Design.

Left: *Befitting this extraordinary bath, a massive wardrobe provides ample storage (and a bit of privacy for the toilet area). The natural graining of the wardrobe's fine hardwood is enhanced with a gleaming protective finish; the top, where condensation might collect, is a thin slab of granite.*

A QUIET, no-nonsense retreat is what these homeowners wanted—and got—in their sophisticated modern master bath. Still, there's an ancient echo here, perhaps of a classical Greek or Roman bath, where contemplation as well as cleanliness was the order of the day. Perhaps it's the unstinting use of pale gray marble. The patrician material shows up in marble tile on the floor and in impressive marble slabs on the tub surround, long vanity shelf, and shower entry. This timeless, luxurious stone makes an important design statement without intruding on the subdued atmosphere. To keep things from becoming heavy, other elements in the room add sparkle, edginess, and humanity. Most notably, the unusual sinks, mounted on black bases that partially hide the plumbing works, offer sculptural interest, while the chrome fittings and small mirrors create a sense of liveliness. The watercolor painting of an idealized residential exterior adds a traditional grace note.

This shower stall facing a row of windows shares a frosted glass wall with one end of the soaking tub, which allows the stall to receive light from two directions. A heavy marble lintel that is part of the same slab on which the marble-framed tub rests helps keep water off the bathroom floor.

Opposite: *In a space that's mostly pale gray and white, the eye is drawn toward the simply framed watercolor over the tub. Artwork depicting an exterior scene, especially one that includes a windowed building, is a clever way to add a vista to the bath. Here, it allows the introduction of a few fresh, yellow-green tints elsewhere.*

WHILE MOST CONTEMPORARY DESIGNS use neutral or primary-plus-white color schemes, this one takes a painterly approach that's downright romantic. A golden glow that's almost Impressionistic suffuses this bath, making it cozy even on the chilliest days. The confident complementary color scheme of yellow and violet is rendered here in a luscious cantaloupe and plum. Used in conjunction with a naturally finished golden maple that's nearly the color of the tiles, the effect is as warm and uplifting as afternoon sunlight. Semigloss walls in tangerine and plum add depth and richness to the color scheme, making the bath look larger without feeling remote. Just the right amount of white keeps the colors from becoming monotonous; fittings and accessories in shiny chrome also add a cool touch that's distinctly contemporary. To create a similar look, choose two adjacent colors you love, and balance them with their opposite colors.

A private toilet compartment offers all the necessities: good lighting, ample closed storage, and the all-important rack for reading material. The low-profile one-piece toilet takes up minimal space.

Opposite: *A pristinely simple pure white sink and light fixtures in the same spirit make a fresh contrast to the colorful surroundings. To the right of the sink, a spacious closed cabinet in mellow maple and a narrow shelf below the frameless, beveled-edge mirror provide ample storage.* Designer: Joy Wilkins, Custom Kitchens by John Wilkins Inc.

A simple maple banquette next to the shower staff snuggles up beneath a small drop-down vanity storage shelf. Above, a good-size window offers ample natural light for applying makeup. The plum-and-gold color scheme is carried through into the adjacent bedroom.

A spacious shower stall tiled in golden hues imparts a warm, pampering air. The shower wall, half tile, half glass, lets the sun shine in while providing a measure of privacy.

Glass block, the mid-20th-century architect's darling that fell from favor, is back in a big way. With today's trend toward putting mammoth houses on small lots on a collision course with our demand for more windows, glass block is likely to become even more popular. Even houses set away from the crowd need some privacy, and for them, glass block proves a beautiful solution, as it does here. In these two bathrooms, textured glass block runs the full height of the bathing area. Greenhouse ceilings above go way beyond the usual skylight to fill the space with brilliant sunlight. Clearly, the natural interplay of sunshine and cascading water creates all the sparkle these spaces need. Allowing natural forms and functions to create design drama this way is in tune with the best contemporary design philosophy. It celebrates a free, spirited, and natural outlook that, in its own way, is timeless.

Left: *Incredibly dramatic, this shower/bath uses the interplay of light and dark, sun and water, to give the owners an experience very like bathing in some mountain grotto. The angled glass block wall brings in diffused light and offers privacy.*

Opposite: *Wooden board beams form a modern-style loggia to cut some of the sun's glare in this glass-enclosed shower. A marble bench, safely out of the spray but within the shower staff area, is a thoughtful touch.*

An ordinary 5×6-foot powder room was transformed into a dramatic jewel of a space with an otherworldly contemporary design. To keep the room visually spacious, branched quartzite from Brazil was randomly placed as the flooring and as the wall accent. (This quartzite is a metamorphic sandstone formed by water and minerals traveling through the capillaries of the stone, creating a unique texture and veins, or dendrites, that appear as "branches" in the stone.) Black granite tiles matching the vanity countertop were also used as flooring to unite all elements of the room. Both the wall stone and the mirror edge were randomly chiseled to create a sense of visual movement. For even more drama, a combination of metallic finishes was applied to the walls, imparting a subtle, gleaming luster. Tiny pendant lights dangle like silver jewelry before the mirror, echoing the sparkle of the stainless-steel sink. This bath is proof you don't need a big space, just a big design concept!

Above: *Repeating the rhythm established by the chiseled tile, the mirror was carefully cut and set into a mahogany wood frame. The frame is bolted into the wall to allow for a 1½-inch gap to enclose incandescent rope lighting, creating extra drama and interest.*

Right: *A stainless-steel sink is cradled in a custom cabinet with a mahogany radius front and hand-forged steel legs. A black granite top was added to complete an elegant, contemporary piece of functional art. To pull the room together, 2×2-inch tiles of the black granite used on the countertop were also used on the floor.*

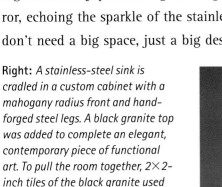

Opposite: *Along the walls, branched quartzite stone from Brazil was chiseled for subtle visual movement. The walls are adorned with a specialty glaze using a combination of metallic finishes.* Designer: Lori W. Carroll, ASID.

Deft and Dazzling

A TRADITIONAL OR TRANSITIONAL SPACE can easily be built up in layers, but a contemporary space needs to be thought through from the ground up, especially if it adheres to a minimalist aesthetic. It's distinctly possible to create a striking contemporary bath in a typical "white box" room, but it's certainly easier if you have the advantage of carving out an interesting architectural shell. Interior designers and architects refer to this process as "getting the bones right first." These two baths testify to the importance of architecture as the structural framework for modern style. In one, a skylight window floods the space with light, and a dramatically angled wall shelters the tub, creating strong areas of light and dark. In a space like this, sculpturally inspired fixtures and mirrors are icing on the cake. In the other bath, every specific need of the owners was anticipated and accounted for in advance, with solutions built into the space.

Left: *Minimalist but not chilly, this pristine bath borrows from the Asian aesthetic as well as a very clean-cut contemporary style. The wall-hung sinks are universally accessible, and the uniquely styled tub is nicely in tune with the classic-modern rattan chair in the window.* Fixtures and fittings: Sottini.

Right: *A home spa with attitude, this bath has cubbyholes and cupboards aplenty to make basic bath storage part of the design of the space rather than something that intrudes on it. Deft touches, including a recessed light strip and unusually shaped windows, add to the interest.* Designer: Leonardo Umansky and Ramiro Diazgranados, Arxis Design Studio.

Fields of strong color played against bright white fixtures is a foolproof recipe for an exciting contemporary space. If your budget is limited, you can make a memorable statement just by painting the walls in one or two of your favorite vivid colors. For the most striking look, choose two widely different colors, such as royal blue and lime; for a more subtle sense of depth, choose two adjacent colors like royal blue and violet or lime and leaf green. Against such strong hues, even the simplest white fixtures gleam with fresh importance. If your budget allows, you can build up the look with installed materials that create pleasing variations on your color theme. These two baths use tiles—some solid-color mosaic, some a mottled mix of related tones—to create depth and interest within a limited color range. Silvery chrome and glass are all you need to complete this artful, modern look.

Left: *Small tiles climb the walls and cover deftly designed corner shelves to provide a quietly dramatic mosaic look. Slightly larger floor tiles and wall paint, all in the same shade of deep blue, create a cocoon-like ambience.* **Fixtures and fittings: Kohler.**

Opposite: *Blues in a range from royal purple to turquoise create dramatic backdrops for the pure white fixtures in this striking bath. But it's the wall and floor tiles, mottled and swirled with silvery blue and violet tones, that really captivate the eye.* **Fixtures and fittings: Sottini.**

IN A RUSTIC ENVIRONMENT, the modern-style emphasis on texture over ornamentation is right at home. This vacation house on a pond in New England is a fine example. It enjoys a richly understated design that pays homage to both the beauty of nature and the modern aesthetic. Its master bath is completely open to the master bedroom, creating a spacious retreat. High, clerestory windows and a central skylight admit an abundance of natural light while preserving the owners' privacy. The design achieves an interesting mix of textures with the smooth-grained maple used for the bath's cabinets and the knotty cedar used for the upper walls and tray ceiling that frames the skylight. It's the room's tiles, however, that really make this space special. Large in size, their ombré tones of deep green, teal, umber, gold, and purple-gray look even richer thanks to their subtly textured, slightly lustrous surface.

Right: *Large slate-textured tiles with a subtle sheen in a rich array of earth tones create natural drama in this bath. A roomy whirlpool tub shares a partition wall with the shower, keeping the overall space uncluttered and letting the beautiful tones of the tile take center stage.*

Opposite: *Fine-grained maple cabinets, knotty cedar walls, and deep-tone tiles create a symphony of natural colors and textures in this masterful bathroom. The drama is enhanced by an artfully positioned skylight that puts the tub area in a natural spotlight.* Architect: Sidnam Petrone Gartner. Tile: Stone Source.

For a homeowner who collects art glass, the bath is a perfect place to show off the versatile beauty of this medium. Throughout this room, glass is used in artful ways. A glass inset in the shower wall, one that would ordinarily be clear or simply textured, becomes a witty element when embellished with square glass "water drops." On the wall above the tub, shallow niches show off art glass perfume bottles as well as organize bath supplies, a *tour de force* that can only be the product of exceptional design intelligence and wit. Handsome wood cabinets offer additional places to display colorful art glass and special silver treasures. Even small touches, such as the distinctive Art Moderne–inspired chrome drawer pulls, contribute to the artful, contemporary look. If you're a collector, if your bath is reasonably large, and if the things you collect can stand up to the ambient moisture of the bathroom, why not make a statement with them?

Above: *Pretty and deceptively delicate-looking, a textured glass shelf (its exposed corner angled for safety) holds a clear glass sink bowl. The effect is one of a large-scale piece of art glass. Distinctive silvery drawer pulls on the adjacent cabinet add to the chic, modern look of the space.*

Left: *Textured glass with a pattern suggesting square water droplets is a witty work of art on the shower wall—just one of the special effects that makes this bath unique. The separate toilet compartment's wall holds a full-length mirror, appropriately positioned next to the dressing vanity.*

Opposite: *Shallow niches tucked into this tub wall create a handsome design on their own and provide some perfect places to stash bath supplies and show off art works. Strategically hung full-length mirrors capture the garden views at one end of the room and bring them into the space's interior.*

WHILE PEACH AND YELLOW are popular bath tints, it takes a certain confidence to use full-strength orange. But balanced by less-assertive tones, orange's outgoing nature really shines. Whether you use a lot of color or a little, hues in the yellow and orange families give a welcome burst of warmth to the stalwart neutrals that dominate many baths. In these two modern rooms, tones of yellow, brown, and orange are used to cozy up black, gray, and white. Colors are brought in with nature's own golden wood tones as well as with paint and a really eye-catching wallcovering. While quite clean-lined and frill-free, neither of these spaces is cold—an important psychological consideration in the bath. What's more, the color orange is enjoying a resurgent popularity it hasn't had for decades, so using it with this much confidence makes these baths seem even more sophisticated and fresh.

Rich orange on the ceiling makes a vivid statement in this contemporary bath. Enhanced by gentler golden tones of wood, the orange is set off by a uniquely raffish white shower curtain and punchy black fixtures and vanity top. The confident color scheme lends real distinction to a small space.

Opposite: *Pale gray makes a fine foil to walls decorated in a rich blend of black, orange, brown, and yellow. The unusual shape of the mirror—curvaceously cut and carefully beveled—is subtly echoed in the generously scaled pedestal sink below it.*

If PRIVACY ISN'T A PROBLEM on your property, why not treat your bath to the same scenic pleasures you give your living room? These homeowners added space from a nearby bedroom and closet to their small existing bath to create a new 8×19-foot bath worthy of its inspiring garden view. The lovely view is made even more inspiring with wonderful framing. A half-round window as long as the soaking tub is a dramatic focal point, its pleasing demi-lune shape evoking the classic curve of Palladian windows but with much more dash. To enhance the spacious effect, the room was given a cathedral ceiling by opening the original into the attic. For an added artistic touch, a band of contrasting-color tiles runs along the backsplash of the vanity and tub and defines an area of the floor. Against the calm taupe ground, this green-and-copper band serves as a blithe reminder of nature's own color scheme just outside the window.

Above: *A clear glass wall is all that separates the shower stall from the adjacent tub, allowing the person showering to enjoy the wonderfully framed woodland view. Taupe tumbled-marble tiles are a handsome counterpoint to the sinuously curved tub.* Tile: Indus Ceramica; shower door: Easco; whirlpool tub: Maax.

Left: *A huge half-round window edged in black is a simple but spectacular frame for a wonderful view. To create a rich, unifying effect, the green-and-copper tile trim of the sink backsplash is repeated along the wall below the window.*

Opposite: *Quiet hues of ivory and pale taupe make a soothing contemporary bath. The double-sink vanity backsplash is enlivened by a custom mural in green and coppery tiles.* Designer: Robert L. Wieland, CKD, CBD, Kitchens by Wieland, Inc. Cabinets: UltraCraft; sinks and toilet: Kohler.

Fearless use of rainbow bright colors makes this one-of-a-kind bath a real stand-out. While bright colors are sometimes used in kids' baths, they're not often poured on over this many surfaces. And they're even less typical in a master bath. For these spirited homeowners, however, a creative approach was the only way to go. While the look is definitely avant-garde, it's carefully thought out. The large multicolored areas are balanced by equally sizable areas of white on walls and inside the shower stall. Pattern, too, somehow softens the intense impact of the colors. Where opaque-painted wood cabinets and a solid laminate tub surround in primary colors could be overwhelming, this bath uses small mosaic tiles separated by white grout and lightly stained wood cabinets that let the grain show. The result is a vibrant, personally expressive space. And, after all, if you can't be yourself in your own bath, where can you be?

Right: *The triangular half-wall in the foreground is deep enough to house a shallow bookcase on the other side. Cabinets and other wood surfaces are stained rather than painted to let the pronounced oak grain show through.*

Left: *Lavishly covered with mosaic tiles in a pattern worthy of Mondrian, the tub surround makes a colorful contrast to the pure white soaking tub. A cleverly designed half-high wall provides a semiprivate area for the toilet. The built-in bookcase is a thoughtful bonus.*

Even the most dramatic contemporary design can benefit from a little wit and a lot of natural beauty, as shown here. Naturally finished golden wood and ragged walls the color of young grass look perfectly appropriate against the dazzling backdrop of glass block and jet black tiles because the whole suite is subordinated to the earthy-colored, unsurpassed drama of the craggy view outside. Glass block, a once-popular staple of midcentury modern design, has escaped its commercial confines and is one of the most beautiful and versatile materials used in modern-style homes today. Here, its place is clearly inspired. Where many people might favor a comfortable lodge look for a mountain eyrie like this, this homeowner, clearly a big fan of modern style, saw something different. While it doesn't reflect the colors or shapes of the great outdoors, this room captures something just as important: the fearless, limitless spirit of the setting.

Right: *A surrealistic custom chair, crafted of tendrilled metal and what looks like a giant leaf, is a witty accent in an already extraordinary master suite. Glimpsed past the pale green colorwashed half wall, the jolt of black tile in the bath beyond looks even more dramatic.*

Opposite: *Heart-stopping vistas of endless mountains are captured in the modern net of a window with heavy grid framing. Curving, full-height walls of glass block echo the geometric theme of the exterior windows and floor tiles, and the round tub seems as mysterious as a pool in deep shade. A small, operable window lets the fresh mountain air inside.*

Minimalist Magic

In a room designed with neutral colors and a minimalist decorating scheme, the accent colors you choose can make a big difference in how the room feels. The owners of a modern, minimalist-style home wanted the same decorating style for their bath but without the chill this look can sometimes impart. Choosing a sophisticated palette of taupe, plum, and silver was an excellent start: The color scheme, largely neutral, is warmer and more interesting thanks to the selection of plum as an accent color. To add more warmth and depth without busyness, the designer had the walls ragged and glazed in layers of taupes and ivories to create an aged, faux-stone impression. The result was an added dimension much more appealing than the previously sterile, white walls. Against the expanse of ivory-white surfaces everywhere, the bright accents of silver and the warm accents of plum and taupe stand out even more dramatically.

Left: *A neoclassically inspired curtain in a luscious taupe shade has a satin sheen, complementing the plum accents and echoing the softly gleaming metallic tones of the room's accessories and fittings.*

Right: *Crystal vases and large pieces of silver-painted pottery add a few dramatic light-reflective elements to this minimalist space, creating interest without too much softness. Pale floor tiles; a textured glass-block window; and frameless, hardware-free cabinetry create a repeated geometric theme.* Designer: Lisa Landry, Decorating Den Interiors.

Modern takes a new turn in a bath where the toilet and bidet are mounted right on the face of the cabinets for the smoothest scheme possible. The wall-hung sink cabinet is coordinated in style but offers a lighter look. Fixtures and fittings: Sottini.

IN A SMALL BATH, beautiful contemporary fixtures and fittings may be the main way to express your modern point of view. But even if your bath is as spacious as these, great modern fixtures can create a pleasing sculptural effect. Fresh tones of lime green and aqua on the walls add to the lively ambience; for a crowning touch, the owners carefully selected pieces of fine contemporary art. To any room, fine art adds a sense of luxury and presence in a way few other elements can. Of course, you wouldn't want to hang a piece of art near the shower, but if your bath has a good exhaust fan and the art is placed well away from water sources, there's no reason why you can't enjoy art in the bath. If you don't have a current collection to choose from, start with an inexpensive print or a local art fair original.

Horizontal lines, a basic element of modern design, make a strong but soothing statement in this bath. The azure blue of the wall behind the tub also contributes to the tranquility of this space. Sculptural modern fixtures with smooth, flowing lines fit in beautifully; umber-colored mirror frames tie in the modern art on the wall. **Fixtures and fittings: Sottini.**

IN A CLUTTERED, busy world, the appeal of minimalism is obvious. Living up to the classic design dictum that everything in the home should be both beautiful and useful, minimalism cuts out the 90 percent of items that aren't. In these two baths, the owners have obviously conquered the impulse to let meaningless "stuff" accumulate. Their challenge was to create decorating schemes that celebrate freedom from clutter without looking cold or uninviting. Both baths utilized tile as a solution: Sleek to look at and easy to care for, tiles epitomize the best of modern design. But because tiles are made from earthen materials and they're as old as civilization itself, tiles also impart a timeless, natural quality that makes a modern aesthetic livable. Interesting textures, varying color tones, and a few nonrectangular shapes really stand out in minimalist schemes like these. In this context, a small row of round tiles makes a friendly statement and a sink bowl appears as a dramatic decorative accessory.

Below: *A splendid array of textured, subtly colored tiles with a slightly metallic sheen has the mesmerizing rainbow effect of oil on water; the peach tone of the concrete provides a subtle contrast. The look is highly dramatic and very natural at the same time.* Designer: Bil Taylor. Tub: Lee Bays Concrete.

Opposite: *Austere and simple, this modern bath evokes a serenity and dignity usually associated with Asian design. The row of decorative bull's-eye tiles beneath the mirror appears quite striking in contrast to the unembellished areas around it.* Tile: Walker Zanger.

A SPIRITED, almost magical ambience brightens this bath. Both playful and regal, the space beguiles with visual puns and parallels that evoke a sort of Disneyland for design-savvy grownups. Cantaloupe, a luscious background color, is reflected in the honey-tone cabinet wood and in an array of gilded and brass accents throughout the room. In cool contrast, an abundance of black-veined white marble is also used. One of the room's many design coups is a frisky mirror-image effect: Frosty white glass tiles are applied to the golden walls, and golden glass tiles are inset into the white marble floor. It's a bold yet carefully thought-out statement that retains its wit by never overstepping its bounds. Equally mesmerizing are the twin vanity sink arrangements: Curved cabinets set with Philippe Starck–inspired saber legs in antiqued copper; rounded marble countertops; and translucent, frosted green sink bowls with the look of found sea glass make the whole affair look as if excavated from Atlantis.

Postmodern style loves to pay tongue-in-cheek homage to design and architectural icons. Here, glass tiles in pearly white march down the walls of this bath in mock Macintosh style, a tribute to the Arts & Crafts icon. Gilded glass tiles inset into the marble floor are a marvelous take on the classic white-tiles-with-black-accents floor.

Opposite: *Honey-hued wood is crafted into curvy cabinets and embellished with the fillip of brass scroll hardware. Sink bowls, frosty green as sea glass; pale, rounded marble countertops; and a dramatic moderne-inspired display niche add to the highly ornamental air.*

Dramatic Dimensions

Wʜɪʟᴇ ᴍᴀɴʏ ᴘᴇᴏᴘʟᴇ would be tempted to turn this generously sized bath into a Renaissance showplace, this owner clearly had something else in mind. The extremely confident minimalist design ends up making even more of all that space. Borrowing concepts from the industrial loft-style design aesthetic, this bath uses a color scheme of high-contrast neutrals and dramatically simple shapes repeated throughout the space. Most of these shapes are curved; notably, the oval black rail around the show-piece tub. Using curved shapes makes a huge difference in giving a stark space an inviting air. This room would have a very different feeling if the tub were enclosed in a square frame and the sink were housed in a squared-off vanity. That's not to say sharper geometrics don't have their place here: The rectangular windows, with their characteristically modern horizontal dividers, admit floods of light. Some might say space and light are among the few real luxuries. This owner clearly agrees.

Left: *This pedestal sink is a striking design, thanks in part to the pristine fittings and the silvery, brushed-metal feet. The sink unit's sharp black-and-white design is excit-ingly set off by the mottled-color, tex-tured wall behind it. A smooth white wall would give an entirely different effect.*

Right: *Meticulously careful placement of every element, from installed fixtures to temporary accessories, is what gives this space its dramatic power. The classic slipper tub looks brand new with its black steel frame and brushed-metal feet.* Fixtures and fittings: Kohler.

Left: *Tub and shower walls are covered in tempered glass and a neutral, 12×12-inch Peruvian stone. The shower floor is made of pebble stones in the same subdued tones.* Designer: Jackie Naylor Interiors. Shower and tub fittings: Kohler.

Above: *His and her vanities made out of centuries-old carved Carrera marble sit under a wall of clerestory windows. Supported by black iron bases, the vanities are 39 inches high to accommodate tall owners.* Marble vanities: Ottoman Treasures; medicine cabinets: Broan; lighting fixtures: Nessen Lighting.

CONTEMPORARY DESIGN can be as cutting-edge or as soothing as you'd like. In this remarkable space, it's both. As befits a second home in the mountains, this master bath pays decorating homage to nature with a mix of bamboo, marble, limestone, and wood. The judicious use of some of man's oldest handiworks—glass and iron—further enhances the timeless, rustic dignity of the space. Limestone stars here, both in the small, painstakingly chiseled 1×3-inch tiles on the wall and in the large crosscut tiles that face the tub. Underfoot, pebble stone floors in the shower and bamboo strip flooring in the rest of the space add to the quiet richness of this sophisticated bath. On the practical side, the custom-height, extra-tall vanities flank a chest-on-chest-style pine cabinet for holding bath supplies. As if all the natural beauty indoors weren't enough, large tempered-glass windows in the tub and shower area open onto a small porch overlooking the mountains.

Glass Act

Right: *This open-plan master bath suite uses a series of translucent glass panels to create a sense of privacy, while enhancing the feeling of light and space.*

Tᴙᴀɴsꜰᴏʀᴍɪɴɢ ꜰᴏᴜʀ ᴄʀᴀᴍᴘᴇᴅ ʟɪᴛᴛʟᴇ ʀᴏᴏᴍs into a light-filled minimalist suite was the task in an apartment of an English Victorian mansion. The new scheme replaces a cluttered pair of bedrooms and bathrooms with a single space, zoned and demarcated by glass walls and internal windows. The bathroom is positioned in one corner of the space. Glass panels, acid-etched so they're translucent but not transparent, were installed above the tub, replacing more traditional window coverings. Using glass instead of traditional opaque wall partitions to divide the space provides intriguing glimpses through to other areas and allows the not-always-plentiful English light to brighten the entire space. The owners' wish, well articulated by the architect, was to have a clean, simple base of stone and glass to set off the varying colors of paintings, cushions, and most of all, flowers and plants.

Opposite: *The mirrored panel above the artful glass sink is actually the front face of a built-in cupboard, while a vertical set of recessed shelving niches is used to display accessories.* Architect: John Kerr, John Kerr Associates. Floor tiles: Tower Ceramics; wood flooring: Junckers; fixtures and fittings: Vola.

M AKEUP COLORS—pink, rose, peach, coral—are wonderful hues for the bath because they throw a flattering wash of color onto skin tones. Many homeowners use these warm, pretty tints with strong neutral colors to balance their intensity, as done here. The contemporary combination of pink, black, and white has a fun 1950's air, but when the materials are opulent marble tiles, the mood is more than fun—it's fabulous. This generously sized bath has room for all the bells and whistles anyone could dream of: a big soaking tub, open storage for everything from towels to a TV, a walk-in shower with a built-in bench, a double sink vanity, a separate room for the toilet and bidet that's as big as many full baths, and even a sauna. In addition to all these built-in features, the bath has plenty of room for uncrowded use of exercise equipment. These homeowners place a high value on good looks and performance—their home's and their own.

Right: *A dramatically angled vanity for two offers maximum storage with style. The angular vanity mirror turns a practical nicety into a dramatic, almost sculptural focal point. Full-length mirrors make it easy to check one's form, any time.*

Above: *Black-and-white marble covers the walls and floor of this luxurious but practical bath, keeping things cool and easy to clean as well as dramatically opulent. A good-size separate shower is conveniently located just a step away from exercise equipment.*

Opposite: *Taking center stage in this dramatic marble exercise room/spa bath, an unabashedly rose pink soaking tub is pure indulgence for homeowners who clearly know what they like.* Designer: Esther Chopp.

MINIMALISM makes a lot of sense in the bathroom. Its lack of physical clutter makes the room safer and easier to use and to clean, and the lack of visual clutter makes the space more serene. In a minimalist bath, the limited number of elements and embellishments stands out all the more dramatically. Two baths in a California home, one a master bath and the other a powder room, express the same minimalist design aesthetic in different ways. In the master bath, the design concept uses a variety of rectangular shapes, from the sinks to the medicine cabinet to the unobtrusive down lights mounted high on the sink wall. In the powder room, round and oval shapes dominate the foreground, contrasting with rectangular forms in the background. The plan is carefully thought out and just as meticulously executed, a necessity for success with a minimalist look.

Left: *Sandstone countertops and tub surround create a mellow stripe effect that relieves the cool plainness of the white walls and minimalist white fixtures. The small bowl-shape sink adds a distinctive look without disrupting the minimalist serenity of the setting.* Designer: Sallie Trout, Trout Studios. Architect: David Cofrances, AIA.

Opposite: *This master bath features medicine cabinets that open when the mirror panel is pivoted sideways in a T-shape configuration, allowing users to access the cabinet's contents and make use of the horizontal mirror at the same time.* Designer: Sallie Trout, Trout Studios. Architect: David Cofrances, AIA.

Like a glamorous movie-star photo or a *film noir* masterpiece of the 1930s and '40s, this Art Deco–style bath sparkles with uptown drama. In addition to black and white, clear acrylic plus clear or mirrored glass are used with calculated abandon throughout the room. All together, they create an environment so lively you don't even miss the lack of color. Little triangular tiles set points-in create the effect of tiny bow ties, a sprightly image that sets the tone for this frisky yet urbane space. Keeping the area from looking too busy, a black-tiled niche makes a simple yet exciting frame for the white porcelain sink and tall mirror. Against this dark-tiled wall, the sparkling geometry of the flanking cabinets looks like crystal jewelry on a black velvet jeweler's cloth. Open shelves above the cabinets show off perfumes and photos.

Opposite: *A classic pedestal sink is framed in black and embellished with sparkling mirror, glass, and acrylic accents all around. Custom light fixtures above the sink and in the center of the room depict man and fish in Matisse-inspired cutouts.*

Left: *Clear cylinders of acrylic held by sparkling metal bands make extraordinary jewel-like drawer pulls on this practical sinkside vanity cabinet. A collection of Art Deco–era toiletries in amber, silver, and faux-ivory lends an extra glamorous touch.*

Tʜᴇʀᴇ's ɴᴏᴛ ᴀ ʙɪᴛ ᴏꜰ ɢʟɪᴛᴛᴇʀ here, but there's lots of gold, thanks to the tawny tones of beautifully finished wood that make this bath so habitable. If you love modern style but not the potentially chilly effect some modern spaces create, take a tip from this bath scheme. Choose cabinets of wood, finished in warm, golden tones, and flooring in complementary earthy shades that feature more brown and tan than black or gray. Add other earthy accents, such as a textured rug in gold, brown, terra cotta, and pumpkin. With a warm base established, you can indulge in mirrors and chrome to your heart's content, and they'll just add sparkle, not coldness. Colors really do affect how we feel, physically as well as emotionally, so in a room where you'll spend a lot of time undressed and wet, creating a cozy ambience is worthwhile!

Right: *A precisely engineered bath cabinet features a full-height drawer/cabinet flanked by twin wall-hung vanity cabinets with undermount sinks. Gooseneck faucets and immediately adjacent towel bars are smart conveniences.*

Opposite: *A vaulted ceiling is a dramatic show-stopper that makes this large bath look even more spacious. The tawny gold tones that distinguish the vanity are echoed in the walls and even in the ceiling so that the warm feeling is not compromised. In a space this warmly hued, an abundance of natural light just amplifies the sunny effect.*

A distinctive vanity whose flowing lines follow the oval shape of the sinks has an Art Deco–inspired air that's both modern and romantic. Classic sink fittings contribute to the sense that this piece is an heirloom from the '30s. Designer: Gabriella Toro, Cippananda Interior Design.

No MATTER how much you admire the clean-lined aesthetic of contemporary design, you'll probably be most comfortable in a bath that coddles you a little bit. This dramatic bath, while unquestionably the height of modernity, still offers some thoughtful comforts as well as thought-provoking design. For one thing, the room feels even more spacious than it is, thanks to splendid views of the great outdoors. If you're lucky enough to have a house with protected, private views, you may want to maximize them with picture windows or even greenhouse windows—bump-out models that have a glass "roof" over the window top to let in even more light. Another appealing feature is the vanity, beautifully crafted in Art Deco–inspired style with all the hallmarks of what's destined to be a modern heirloom. Even if scenic views and custom-crafted vanities are not in your plan, you can still create a modern-style haven in your bath by keeping things simple.

Below left: *A cleverly designed tub surround includes a two-tiered shelf with space for display above and room for stashing bath supplies below. The greenhouse-style window acts as a great light scoop and offers a fine view of the secluded garden.*
Below right: *A separate compartment houses a urinal as well as a conventional low-profile toilet; conveniently located glass shelves provide ample storage space.*

Rhythm and Blue

JUST IMAGINE coming in on a hot day from the garden or the tennis court and splashing cool water on your face in this bath, and you'll know the essence of refreshment. Exquisitely engineered in virtually every detail, this deceptively simple-looking room has a lot more going for it than immediately meets the eye. Green glass, a durable but delicate-looking material, is beautiful and practical for the vanity top and door and creates a pleasing "watery" image most appropriate for a bath. Beautiful blues—cobalt and turquoise—continue the water image and add depth to the scene. Thoughtful details have been chosen for maximum function and elegant form. Notable examples are the curvy, shiny wall radiators that heat up the setting's style appeal while they warm up the room. Niches cut into the wall and vanity base function as cubbyhole storage—and add a little more zip to the architecture.

Above: *A combination of curved and straight lines adds a subtle rhythm to this blue-and-white bath and keeps the minimalism from becoming too stark. A green glass door and coordinating vanity counter provide subtle color and luster.*

Right: *A sparkling stainless-steel sink is a dazzling focal point to the softly glowing green glass countertop. Above, a good-size mirror pulls the intense turquoise blue of the tub area into the room, adding more color in an intriguing way.*

Opposite: *If you remember radiators as ugly, clunky things, you'll scarcely recognize the sleek, shining, almost musical elements that decorate the walls of this bath and tub area. About all these dazzlers have in common with the old radiators is that they're made of metal.* Architect: John Kerr, John Kerr Associates.

Modern designs seem most successful when they take maximum advantage of what contemporary style stands for: a free-spirited, aesthetically honest, and technologically savvy approach to creating an environment for living. In this space, a fresh green-and-white color scheme couldn't be simpler; sparked with a few metallic accents, it's youthful and interesting without being overly dramatic. Perhaps the most remarkable element in this bath is one of the least obtrusive: the toilet. A European design, this wall-hung toilet is height-adjustable, making it comfortable for taller users. The plumbing works are built into the wall, so it's best suited for a renovation or new construction rather than a simple fixture-replacement project. The rest of the suite carries through this clean-lined, elegantly simple design. And the look isn't limited to contemporary settings: Since bathroom fixtures as we know them didn't exist during most historical periods, you may prefer these unobtrusive models even in a traditional décor.

Left: *Spring green and white make a fresh and simple color scheme for a comfortable modern bath. For the ultimate in clean-cut design, the height-adjustable toilet's tank is built right into the wall, saving up to 9 inches of room and making the sleekest possible visual statement.*
Fixtures: Geberit Manufacturing, Inc.

Right: *An oval pedestal sink makes a sleek, pleasingly sculptural statement in any contemporary bath. The trio of hanging lights takes up little space but sheds a lot of light on the subject. With nicely designed fixtures and coordinated fittings, it takes only a few accents, some in color and some metallic, to complete a sparkling decorative scheme.*

A TOWNHOUSE in Greenwich Village designed for a composer, an artist, and their son honors both the family's Japanese heritage and its hectic travel-heavy lifestyle with a serenely modern aesthetic. The couple wanted to indulge in their tradition of taking long, soaking baths but also wanted a separate shower and a double-sink vanity. The architect obliged with a soaking tub joined to the shower in interlocking units to save space. A soothing palette was achieved with faux-limestone facing on the tub surround and shower walls that complement the slate floor tiles and light maple cabinetry. The maple itself was chosen to match the woods used elsewhere throughout the home, a detail that further enhances the feeling of flowing continuity. To bring in more light, so important to eliminating that closed-in feeling, a light shaft, two stories high, takes the idea of a skylight to a whole other level.

Above: *The tub surround projects into a frameless shower to form a small ledge that the two fixtures share, an engineering tactic that made a 5-foot-4-inch tub and separate shower possible in the limited space.*

Left: *Pocket doors at either end of the bath keep the room visually simple and the limited floor space unobstructed. To further streamline the space, medicine cabinets, mirrors, and shelves are frameless and built into walls.*

Opposite: *To minimize the visual impact of the double sinks, a wall-hung vanity appears to float over the floor. A wall-hung toilet produces a similar effect. Overhead, a skylight also helps create a more spacious, open feeling.*
Architect: Sidnam Petrone Gartner. Manufacturer: Stone Source.

MODERN STYLE may look simpler than traditional style, but the best modern looks aren't about cutting out ornamentation. Instead, they're about making every element in a space functionally beautiful. This bath proves the point admirably with a carefully engineered array of delightful elements to be discovered. While not disturbing the purity of the room's mostly rectangular lines, the design offers visual enticements through different media. Mosaic tile, for example, plays a starring role by bringing in luscious yet soothing color plus texture. The tile floor in the round shower stall beguiles further with a stylized design that evokes windswept flowers in a sharp, abstract way. In another allusion to nature, a ribbon of green glass, etched to recall a slender waterfall, gives bathers something appealing to gaze at. A naturally finished wood vanity cabinet topped by a tall, narrow mirror adds warmth and sparkle. The overall effect: clearly chic yet soothing.

Above: *A tall, narrow mirror is enhanced by a frame of small green mosaic tiles that relate to other strong vertical rectangles in the room's design. A vanity cabinet of precisely crafted wood is a sleek piece in the best modern tradition.*

Right: *Look closely, and you'll see the design of windblown flowers made of mosaic tiles decorating this bath's round shower stall floor. Green mosaic tiles, white stone, and naturally finished wood add to the soothing ambience.*

Opposite: *A bathtub framed in stone gains added interest from a tall, curved wall section covered in green mosaic tiles and punctuated by a slender ribbon of inset etched glass. The band of glass has the witty effect of a cascading waterfall.* Designer: Daniel Hopwood, Daniel Hopwood Studio.

THESE MODERN BATHS owe a lot to their extremely careful engineering. Just any no-frills space won't do: These baths are animated by a strongly architectural spirit that considers all the angles, visually as well as functionally. Not all the angles are sharp ones, however. The slipper tub, for example, shows what throwing a curve can do to give a space more appeal. The small, rounded vanity sink has much the same impact in less space. Curves, like wood tones, bring another bonus to modern design: They have the effect of upping the comfort quotient, both visually and physically. If you admire this look but your plans don't include the services of a top-flight modernist architect, do the next-best thing: Think like an architect yourself. Remember the modernist axiom, "form follows function," and think carefully about the simplest way to achieve the functions you need. If you're on a budget, the downside of minimalist modern is that you can't gussy up the place with decorative add-ons. The upside, however, is that simply styled, hard-working fixtures, fittings, furniture, and accessories abound in all price ranges.

Left: *Austere and dramatic, this bath depends on a few big gestures made even more dramatic with pin-spots and other theatrical lighting units placed strategically in the room.*

A deftly designed run of pristine, frameless vanity cabinets is punctuated only by a narrow wooden hamper unit. The hamper uses wood for its breathable quality; a small handhold also provides ventilation with style.

Precisely honed edges build up the geometries of this suite's rigorously minimalist design. Naturally finished wood tones are sparked with lots of white and other pale tones and punctuated by brisk black.

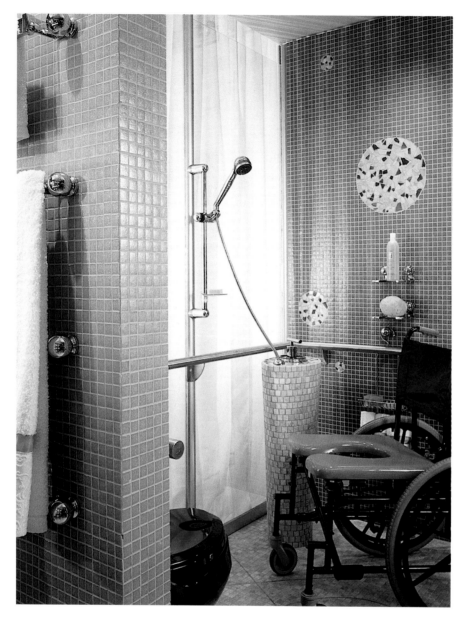

This roll-in shower, tiled in happy tones, is fun and spacious enough for any user. The easy-grip faucet is mounted on a mosaic-tiled, safely rounded column in the floor that rises to chair height. The shower-head, mounted on a sliding bar that can be fixed at any comfortable point, can also be used as a hand-held shower.

YELLOW AND GREEN, nature's most bright and hopeful colors, work nicely together in this bath that proves universal accessibility can go hand-in-hand with style. The citrus tones lend a cheery, youthful air, while the neutral tones of cabinets and countertops offer a soothing counterpoint. This savvy space features a double vanity with counters and sinks at two heights, and instead of fixed storage below that might get in the way, the cabinets roll on casters. Gooseneck faucets and wing-handled controls add to the free-spirited look. Even small, practical details contribute to the good looks of this space: Satin-finished grab bars mounted all around the shower stall make a gleaming, useful accent; similar bars hold towels on the front of the vanities. Other colors and finishes could be used to create a more traditional atmosphere, but these elements and ideas are all adaptable to just about any bath. And that's the real beauty of accessibility!

Opposite: *Vanity countertops at two heights accommodate homeowners with different needs; the lower sink would work for a child or a wheelchair user. Easy-to-operate wing-handled faucets are graceful as well as helpful. Below, two-drawer wood cabinets on casters move with ease wherever they're needed.* Fixtures and fittings: Kohler.

CONTEMPORARY DESIGN is right at home in these master baths, thanks to the lavish use of top-flight materials: beautifully grained marble, glass in clear sheets and textured blocks, large mirrors, and sparkling chrome. Except for the marble, already long in use when ancient Greece was the latest thing, all these materials are quintessentially modern. In fact, large expanses of mirror and glass have come to exemplify contemporary style, with its spirit that will admit no limits. To keep these cool, smooth surfaces from reading a bit chilly or hard, both these baths employ some strategic warm-ups. In one, blonde wood, ample access to natural light, and some artfully designed lighting fixtures offer a balancing warmth. In the other, a softly hued beige marble, a few flowering plants, and a dash or two of regal violet color create an inviting ambience. In both spaces, the overall impression is one of sparkle, spirit, and unabashed luxury.

Below: *Users gazing into this infinity of mirrors cannot help but be beguiled by the magic of the room's design. The juxtaposition of glass block with a delicately veined marble is a master stroke that makes the walls seem to undulate, further enhancing the otherworldly sense of the place.* **Opposite:** *White marble with dramatic black and gray veining gives this bath an extraordinary presence beyond its size. The shower stall, with its easily accessible handheld shower, built-in marble seat, and skylight, is both practical and beautiful. Softening the effect of all this stone, blonde wood creates an appealing contrast.*

Transparent and translucent glass give a sparkling performance in this minimalist modern bath. An ingeniously designed glass wall and door leads from the major part of this bath to the toilet compartment beyond. A separate toilet compartment with a door that closes is predicted by some to be tomorrow's most-wanted bathroom luxury. This bath already has it, but it's clearly not some claustrophobic closet. The bathing area features a stone-tiled tub that overlooks a window as wide as the tub and its surround, offering a sense of expansiveness. The wide, flat surround gives bathers a safe, easy-to-use perch while getting in and out of the tub—a thoughtful touch that's easy to plan in but not so easy to add on later. Careful orchestration of textures, tones, and volume/mass, a hallmark of professional design, is a special challenge in a minimalist, modern space. When the orchestration works, you may not know how the effect was achieved, but you can definitely tell that it does.

Right: *A private toilet compartment is secluded, but not boxed in, behind a glass wall and door that are frosted halfway up. Paneling and a coordinating frameless vanity cabinet feature an interesting tiger-maple stripe pattern that adds subtle interest to the space.*

Opposite: *Here, matte, textured stone contrasts with the smooth sparkle of the granite vanity countertop and the spacious window. The lowest third of the window wears a simple vertical shade for bathing privacy, while the rest is left clear to capture the view and lend an expansive feeling to the space.*

WHETHER THE MOOD they strike is dramatic and formal or simple and serene, contemporary-style baths are visually sleek, not cluttered. To many busy homeowners, these are the most restful settings of all. But to make the minimalist modern look work, adequate closed storage is essential. This is often no small task, given the number of less-than-photogenic items most bathrooms have to stash. Vanities in these two rooms, although very different in mood, offer the necessary storage to keep clutter under wraps. These vanity cabinets do much more, too: They do a great job of articulating the design statement in a setting with very few props or accessories to rely on. Playing supporting roles, luxurious natural flooring, simple yet interesting windows, and good-size mirrors hung in artful, sometimes unexpected places offer functional basics with cool good looks. Look for items of this caliber through your interior designer or architect or, occasionally, at your local home store.

Left: *Blonde wood and lots of white give this bath an invigorating air of pristine freshness. Cabinets and shelves that look inspired by Swedish modern furniture offer a useful combination of open and closed storage, all of it easily accessible.*

Opposite: *Who says a double-sink vanity has to be the same on both ends? This unique vanity design is worthy of the dramatic sculptural environment of this bath. The clever shape offers the light scale of a wall-hung sink, the storage of a vanity sink, and even a measure of safety by providing a handhold at the bathtub steps.*

WHILE FIXTURES are available in virtually any color today, white is still the overwhelmingly preferred color. Some consumers will choose white fixtures even if they're installing very colorful permanent tiles as backgrounds, so the popularity of white fixtures isn't due solely to practicality. One of the reasons white remains right in so many homeowners' minds is obviously that "white goes with everything." White fixtures look peaceful against pale blue walls today, brilliant against burgundy red ones tomorrow. But even if you commit to a strongly colored wall in a permanent material, white fixtures still give you maximum leeway to change your scheme. The same pale blue plus white that looks young and fresh with lime green towels and accessories will appear sharply sophisticated with black towels and accessories. Another reason white fixtures may be retaining their appeal is even more simple: Traditional or modern, the shapes of bath fixtures just stand out more interestingly in white!

Right: *Pale aqua and the creamy tones of naturally finished wood are a perennially popular color scheme that looks especially well against these pristine white fixtures.* Manufacturer: Ideal Standard.

Opposite: *Tiles, large and small, in warm and cool colors, create an energetic background for the all-white fixtures and white walls in this bath.*

Creative Contrasts

AN EXCEPTIONAL VIEW of the great outdoors was the inspiration for a bath that's unquestionably modern but not at all chilly or utilitarian. Dreamy, tawny tones wrap the homeowners in a pampering ambience, while an artful mix of materials provides rich visual interest in a subtle way. In virtually every case, the designer sidestepped the usual solutions in favor of quietly dramatic, fresh ideas. On the window wall, the unusual tub surround of lapped wood strips replaces the expected marble tiles to create a restful, horizontal pattern. In the semi-enclosed shower area, clear glass and more marble tiles were passed over in favor of a ceiling-high panel of frosted glass that contrasts with pebbled walls. The mix of smooth and textured, dark and light, and glass and metal elements continues throughout the room. The result is a pleasing balance that's both soothing and energizing.

Left: *Strong architectural statements abound in this one-of-a-kind bath. The smooth, frosted glass wall that divides the shower from the rest of the bath is an exciting contrast to the pebbled shower walls.*

Opposite: *High style that's also practical: Here, a pair of vanity sinks presents a compact profile but has practical little wings to hold toiletries. Slender tube lights flank the large mirrors in the preferred position for clearest vision.*

With a view like this, the designer wisely kept interior gestures subdued. The exception is a beautiful floor, tub surround, and vanity top made of rose, white, and taupe-gray striated marble. In those rare instances when the outdoor view fails to engage the bather, a TV built into the mirrored end wall is available.

Opposite: *When privacy's not an issue and the view is spectacular, who could blame a homeowner who removes as many barriers as possible to the great outdoors? This soaking tub makes the most of a spectacular vista with a vast picture window and a large-size skylight, too.*

Most people fortunate enough to have a glorious view of trees and mountains would orient a living room or bedroom to the setting. This home goes a bit further, giving its generously sized bath a comfortable front-row seat to the ever-changing scene. Since the soaking tub is where a person would most likely spend leisure time, it's given pride of place next to the window and beneath the skylight. Mirrored end walls give the view even greater emphasis. What's nicest about this bath, however, is that it's attractive enough to make a splash in just about any contemporary-style home. If the view weren't this marvelous and the picture window was simply a plain or mirrored wall, the room would still be enviable. Clean lines, lots of expansive unframed mirrors, and a drop-dead-gorgeous surfacing material like this rosy marble add up to a look that can play a starring or secondary role with equal savoir faire.

TRANSITIONAL STYLES are just that: transitions between traditional and contemporary styles. Many of today's most exciting rooms are expressions of transitional designs, born of the tension between old and new, ornate and clean-cut, romantic and edgy. But transitional style is more than just exciting. It can also be very practical because it fearlessly borrows options from both traditional and contemporary venues. In transitional styles, you'll see rustic or elegant looks that span centuries but are united by one or more strong design elements: perhaps a repetition of colors or patterns that cleverly create a mood. You'll also see rustic and elegant elements combined, again most successfully when they share a bond of color or mood. In transitional styles, the most modern fixtures may keep company with tiles that were modern in the days of the Caesars, and brand-new designs inspired by ecology meet up with those inspired by nature 100 years ago. Sophisticated yet very livable, transitional styles will get you where you live!

ECLECTIC

If you love to travel and appreciate a sophisticated scheme that can't be easily pigeonholed, you may be drawn to the wit and dignity of eclectic style. A deft blend of antique and modern, practical and inspirational, eclectic takes the best from many eras. A great eclectic look might be a traditional-style vanity in fine cherry or mahogany with a

A riot of colorful tiles appears surprisingly livable, thanks to the balanced color scheme of red, blue, and yellow. An antique mirror, tub, and gilt corbels in wall corners look perfectly at home with the sculptural modern sink in this clever eclectic bath.

modern, art-glass countertop sink and sparkling modern light fixtures in metal and glass. Another might be a massive, traditional pedestal sink with contemporary-style fittings and lots of mirrors or a stainless-steel counter atop a Shaker-style wood vanity.

For unusual storage in a generously sized bath, consider a French country armoire or an Asian cabinet. A mix of natural or ethnic-inspired materials—marble, granite, ceramic tiles that look like tumbled marble, terra-cotta, or ethnic-patterned tiles—is handsome and timeless; wrought-iron pulls, handmade baskets, and other ethnic touches are nice embellishments for your eclectic bath. What works with everything: Asian art and textiles that celebrate nature in a stylized way, such as batiks; wood shutters or matchstick blinds; glass and glass-look acrylic pulls and accents; rich neutrals (ebony, ivory, mahogany); a few jewel-tone colors; and shapes that are either pared way down or flawlessly crafted. Here's the place for that African basket, Chinese lacquer tray, modern black-and-white photo, and Shaker cabinet.

ARTS & CRAFTS/MISSION

Handsome Arts & Crafts and Mission styles offer modern simplicity and traditional warmth and celebrate the handmade and artisan-crafted. More cerebral than the cabin look, more contemporary than American country, Arts & Crafts/Mission style is great in bungalows, lodge-style houses, and anywhere a rustic yet creative style is wanted. To create the look in your bath, reach for rich, dark, earthy colors—mustard, bottle green, wine, paprika, chocolate, and spice brown. Mission style is fairly easy to find in cabinets today, especially in oak, so

find one and top it with a counter in tumbled-marble tiles, slate, or, best of all, ceramic tiles in stylized patterns and earthy colors. Except for Mediterranean, no other style makes so much use of handmade, hand-painted tiles, so if you can't use them everywhere, use plain ceramic tiles for the most part and lavish decorative tiles on the backsplash, chair rail, and countertop border. For more Arts & Crafts/Mission elements, specify bronze or wrought-iron hardware and wallcoverings in stylized leaf and flower motifs (oak leaves, acorns, ivy, tulips, and anything by Arts & Crafts founder William Morris). For accents, clue into colorful pottery, wooden bowls, and hand-glazed ceramic tiles.

Who couldn't use a little more serenity and balance in his or her life? This Asian-inspired bath delivers both in simple abundance. Precise craftsmanship and careful placement of each element in the space create a peaceful retreat. Windows: Andersen Windows, Inc.

A reinterpretation of the classic Asian stacked cabinets makes a handsome, appropriate addition to this bath's storage. Open shelving with pull-out rattan baskets enhances the exotic yet dignified look.
Cabinets: Decorá.

ETHNIC FLAIR

Rich elements from many cultures go into the exotic mix of this style. A more down-to-earth cousin of urbane eclectic style, Ethnic Flair goes global and comes on strong in the new millennium. Start with a neutral foundation like textured white plaster or mottled stone-look tiles and a dark, distressed-wood vanity cabinet topped in stone or faux-stone counters. This look was made for the new sink bowls in hammered metal or art glass that sit entirely on top of the counter: Pair one with a primitive-style gooseneck faucet and inventive fittings in antiqued brass or brushed nickel. Add practical terra-cotta tile flooring; a simple, in-floor shower area; and Roman shades or tent-flap-style window coverings in plain muslin or ethnic-patterned textiles. For color schemes, take inspiration from native textiles. Choose paprika, ebony, ivory, spice brown, and gold in bold chevron patterns, jewel-toned paisleys, brilliant silk sari hues, or whatever handsome hand-loomed look strikes your fancy. Stick to a few high-impact decorative accessories: hammered, enameled brass; wrought iron; earthenware; wooden bowls; and woven baskets (but avoid Babel). In addition to ethnic patterns, you can select motifs from the natural world—whimsical frogs, elegant herons, dignified elephants, and tropical flowers and foliage—that affirm ecological awareness. Just for fun, scout out artifacts devised of recycled industrial products, a hallmark of inventive local cultures around the world.

A breezy ambience coexists beautifully with opulent touches in this upscale, beach-inspired bath. Shells, pussy-willow branches, and other natural accents are right at home with marble tile and a flattering palette of taupe, ivory, and shell pink. Designer: Sandra Steiner-Houck, CKD, Sandra Steiner-Houck, CKD, Inc.

BEACH HOUSE

While not strictly a style, waterfront schemes in the bath are so popular they warrant mention on their own. The affinity of water with bathrooms is a natural, so it's no wonder so many bathroom schemes feature images of the sea, such as boats, shells, fish, an so on. The shell-shocked beach look has become a 1950's cliché, however, so it takes a bit of thought to render the concept freshly. If you like traditional style, American country, English country, Mediterranean, and lodge/cabin lend themselves to the beach cottage look. Whitewashed walls and cabinets, a classic blue-and-white palette, and a very few, carefully chosen, vintage accessories such as carved wooden shore birds or sailboats do the job nicely. A more opulent traditional bath might utilize formal, neoclassical shell motifs, perhaps with an 18th-century color palette of ivory, shell pink, and taupe. If you like contemporary style, California Spa is easy: Whites, the neutrals of driftwood and sea sponges, and sea-glass blue-green accents bring the look home.

In any of these settings, natural shells used in moderation are lovely, but don't be tempted to "improve" them with dyes, glue, or flowers. A large conch or sawtooth clamshell is great to hold soaps; a clear, heavy brandy snifter filled with the very best finds from family beach vacations recalls happy memories.

N ATRIUM in an old chateau, jazzed up with a few witty postmodern touches—that's the atmosphere in this unusual but very seductive bath. A mix of green, mauve, and neutral-tone tiles in both polished and matte slate textures are masterfully blended for a subtly rich effect. The room has an enviable sense of pacing: Special touches, like a few hand-painted botanical tiles, are set where they can be discovered almost accidentally rather than being placed where you can't help but see them. There's an offhanded elegance and a quiet confidence about this approach that's as much sensed as seen. To keep things from becoming too subtle, a few grand design touches enliven the space with forthright drama. The full-length self-patterned draperies are purely theatrical, and the mirrored wall mounted with minimalist sinks is a master stroke of modernism. The giant neo-classical urned topiary is a grand gesture in keeping with this inspired space.

Left: *A subtle palette of gray-green, dusty lilac, and taupe tones lends an antique, romantic air to this spacious bath. Bands of the signature colors give postmodern pizzazz to the shower area; an ottoman upholstered in dusty mauve "tiles" is a witty addition.* **Right:** *A mix of highly polished moss green tiles on the tub surround and weathered slate-look green tiles on the floor creates a sense of depth and complexity without a lot of fuss. Floor tiles are a blend of subtle tones: dusty mauve, tan, chartreuse, and gray as well as antique green. A few hand-painted botanical tiles are delightful discoveries.*

STYLE CONSIDERATIONS **239**

Streamlined yet Seductive

IF YOU LIKE the look of transitional style, create it easily with lots of white. Sleek modern fixtures can look at home with curvy traditional cabinetry if you choose them in white and pale neutral tones. In the baths shown here, white predominates, cloaking all with a clean yet very romantic aura. The only other tones in the room are undemanding neutrals: the tan of a wicker basket; the soft brown of a weathered wood armoire; the deeper, lustrous brown of wood strip flooring. The great things about this concept are that white paint is easy to come by at all price points and white tiles and fixtures are typically less expensive than colored or decorated tiles (although white fittings may cost more than chrome ones). Best of all, the unity provided by white somehow makes everything go together, regardless of how disparate their origins or styles may be. Chic and peaceful, white is right.

Right: *This room's focal point is a curvaceous French country armoire that stashes everything from a portable TV to designer bed and bath linens. The distressed wood tones of the armoire help relieve the room's monochromatic color scheme.* **Fixtures: American Standard.**

Traditional raised-panel cabinets look surprisingly in sync with a modern sink above them. What they have in common are great lines and a pure white color.

A GUEST BATHROOM in the century-old home/studio of a prominent painter/sculptor was given an artistic treatment of its own during a recent major renovation. The room is a transitional-style treasure, incorporating Gilded Age grandeur and Italian modernism in a surprisingly serene enclave. As you'd expect when the client himself is an artist, every innovative detail was planned with extreme care. The owner wanted the space to feel contemporary but without up-to-the-minute materials or design clichés. His wish was to blend old and new as artfully as possible—a request with which the architect happily complied. The spectacular sink and extra-long cast-iron tub, all the more impressive because they're vintage originals, joined a few judiciously chosen new elements, including the glass shelf and towel bar. For the surfacing materials, a color scheme of aqua, antique gold, and rich brown was chosen for its timeless appeal.

Ancient design elements include walls hand troweled with ocher-tinted plaster and a handsome sink with a fluted-column pedestal. Halogen lights piercing the wall punctuate the space with modern touches.

Opposite: *Turquoise bath tile may be a cliché—but not here. These industrial-grade Italian floor tiles are randomly cut in trapezoidal shapes and splayed like a starburst from the room's center point. Similar square and rectangular tiles are used on the shower wall.* Architect: Sidnam Petrone Gartner. Tiles: Stone Source.

THESE TWO TRANSITIONAL-STYLE BATHS borrow the best from contemporary and traditional designs and mix them deftly, for timeless results. The secret to a transitional-style room's success is to make sure every element the user can see or touch is of good quality. Careful editing of elements is especially important in rooms that share a clean-lined aesthetic because each detail in the space really stands out. In both of these baths, carefully chosen fixtures, fittings, and accessories function almost as works of art, providing visual and tactile appeal. It helps that, in these two rooms, the "shell" is opulent without being ornate. So if marble or custom tiles are beyond your budget, look for wallcoverings with a sophisticated faux finish. Walls that are inherently attractive on their own make the best backgrounds for other beautiful elements, whether they're a crystalline green-glass sink bowl, a curvy faucet, a mass of beeswax candles, or a group of gleaming silver toiletry bottles.

Cool and otherworldly, this bath owes a lot of its dreamy quality to the softly gleaming metallic tile wall surfaces. Sculptural fixtures, from the glass sink bowl to the one-piece low-profile toilet, are beautifully modern. The raised-panel lower walls provide traditional balance.

Opposite: *Open wrought-iron shelving units with a classical obelisk shape are practical and sophisticated. Their airy look balances the traditional dark wood tub surround and vanity cabinet, keeping the room from looking too heavy. A frameless shower door adds contemporary simplicity.*

ORIGINAL MURALS on canvas depicting scenes of the forest and sea pay homage to the great outdoors in this magnificent bathroom. Stained glass, cherry millwork, sophisticated black fixtures, and other artful elements also play starring roles in the richly embellished space. Adjacent to the mirror above the pedestal sink, custom-designed stained glass depicts animals and oak leaves and is back-lit for added drama. (Custom stained glass is appearing in more baths of all sizes as an artful alternative to window coverings.) The shower wall features hand-glazed putty-colored tiles repeating the theme of woodland animals and oak leaves. Custom-designed cherry wood millwork used throughout the bath is all stained to match a woodgrain vinyl floor installed on the diagonal. If you're on a budget but your heart is set on a custom mural, consult a nearby art school; if the historical look of murals is what you're after, wallcovering versions are also available.

Opposite: *A suite of gleaming black porcelain fixtures adds the necessary dash of drama to this spacious, soothing personal environment. The antique-looking rug and wood armchair provide an extra measure of comfort, in character.* Designer: Robert E. Lewcock, ASID, Zimmerman Design Group. Fixtures: Kohler; chair: Milling Road.

Right: *A separate toilet compartment and a curtained alcove for the spacious bathtub are each given the royal treatment in this handsome bath. Custom-painted murals depicting forest and seagoing themes raise the whole look to an aristocratic level.* Tile: Ann Sacks Tile & Stone; murals: Timothy Haglund Studio; flooring: Wilsonart.

Classically elegant yet youthful and romantic, this bath is a beautiful example of the enduring power of white-on-white as the color scheme for a bath. Any space will be visually expanded with an all-white scheme, but it's the special touches, both architectural and decorative, that really define this bath as special. Most spectacular is the rotunda that houses the whirlpool tub and floods the room with light. Curved walls and windows are rather extraordinary, but the overall effect is wonderfully serene rather than striking. Another quietly remarkable element is the cornice of traditional crown and dentil mouldings made of small tiles rather than carved wood. Like the rotunda, these mouldings recall architectural motifs begun in ancient Greece and revived throughout history, including our own 18th-century Federal period. If these architectural elements aren't in your plans, you can still create a serene and romantic effect with walls, floors, and fixtures all in white, sparkled with an array of brilliant, pretty accents. Find a vintage frameless mirror with beveled edges, pick up some old silverplate at a flea market, and go to town!

Above: *Subtle and beautiful, white-on-white dimensional tiles embellish the walls of this classically inspired shower stall. A clear glass door affords a view over the tub into the great outdoors beyond.*

Left: *A Venetian glass mirror creates a magical effect in this bath that's built on a subtle range of white tones. A traditional pedestal sink and a small butler's cart show off vintage silver accessories and recall the ambience of a European hotel.*

Opposite: *A classic rotunda-shape bathing alcove gains added beauty thanks to tall windows overlooking a pretty view. Mosaic tiles in mostly pale tones pave the steps to the tub.*

MANY SUCCESSFUL TRANSITIONAL SCHEMES are created by using soothing neutrals through-out, but that's not the only way to go. If you crave the emotional rush only beautiful, intense color can provide, why not indulge it in a room as personal as your bath? This room pairs vivid lime green, the signature color of millennium-modern style, with a refined, traditional blue. It's a mix that's energizing but not jarring. One savvy detail is that the modern green color shows up on the plain wall, while the traditional blue appears on the classically paneled wall. It's almost as if the designer chose this way to demonstrate how happily new and old can coexist together. Other elements that make the concept work are easy to adapt, such as consistent use of traditional-style fixtures and a black-and-white tile floor in a timeless pattern. Why not choose a two-color com-bination you love, and go for it? You'll have the freshest bath on the block!

Right: *Frisky rows of mosaic tiles in watercolor tints of green, blue, and lilac are as sprightly and modern as a Chagall, and they're especially pretty next to the Wedgwood blue wall with its traditional molding panels. A simple pine-framed mirror lets the bright lime wall play a starring role.*

Left: *Dazzling lime green is not for the faint-hearted, but it can certainly put a zing in your morning ritual! Below the chair-rail level, the room is comfortably grounded with a fine French blue that subtly enhances the traditionally paneled wall. Fixtures and flooring in white, black, silver, and wood create a cool, calm counterbalance to the vivid green wall.*

TWO MOODS OF COMFORT are expressed in these spacious spa-size baths. One is rustic and rather contemporary; the other is more polished and traditional but still includes the surprise of a few rough elements for contrast. Although their overall looks are very different, they share key design elements that are dependably successful. The mix of carefully chosen neutral tones—white, cream, tan, and brown—is unfailingly warm and calming. When these hues are rendered in luxurious natural materials such as wood and marble, they're rich and timeless, too. Both rooms also feature a fixture that has become basic to today's luxury bath: a king-size whirlpool tub framed in marble. Most importantly, both baths take maximum advantage of the sunlight and views that lie just outside these private retreats. Studies continue to affirm that natural light and nearby greenery offer significant health benefits as well as being beautiful. So if privacy's not a problem, let the sun shine in!

Left: *Opulent, caramel-colored marble and two-story log poles may seem an unusual combination, but their mellow tones work together to create the sense of an aristocratic forest lodge. A row of casement windows topped by transom windows makes a handsome frame for the woodsy view beyond.* Builder: Rocky Mountain Log Homes.

Right: *Slatted Swedish chairs are the perfect place to lounge after enjoying the whirlpool tub, shower, or sauna. The log walls and a long row of French doors spanning the length of the room serve to link the spa with the great outdoors.* Builder: Rocky Mountain Log Homes.

Stripes are one of the most versatile design tools available, easily able to look both formal and high-spirited at the same time. The same can be said for deep evergreen: A color especially in vogue during Edwardian times, it's dramatic and chic yet surprisingly warm. In these two baths, stripes in a deep black-green are paired with other tones for two very different, sophisticated effects. In one bath, the black-green pairs with bright white on a show-stopping ceiling that brings to mind a gaily striped cabana tent. Precision cutting and placement pays off in a wonderfully confident result. In the other bath, deepest evergreen alternates with a slightly lighter bottle green for a different dimensional effect. This somewhat simpler treatment nevertheless gives the bath's fixtures and accessories a dramatic emphasis. Here, the precision involved is careful planning and hanging of the artworks. With or without a generous budget, these crisp schemes make a great impression.

Below: *High casement windows gain added importance framed above and below by professional black-and-white photos with wide white mats. Against the formally striped dark wallcovering in two shades of hunter green, the white elements stand out dramatically. To keep the look from becoming too predictable, a few jolts of crimson spark the setting.*

Opposite: *A green so dark it's almost black is a sophisticated mate to white in this bath's lively, tent-inspired ceiling and walls. Tawny taupe marble exerts a soothing influence. The generously scaled window gives bathers an unobstructed view of the completely enclosed yard, where the play of light and shadow echoes the dark-and-light scheme of the bath itself.*

A 10×11-FOOT BATH isn't small by most standards, but it's not vast, either. To create an arresting design statement in a less-than-lavish footprint, this room uses a minimalist approach with just a few quality elements thoughtfully deployed. If you like the look of minimalist chic, this bath features ideas you can use to your advantage—even if you're working with a typical 5×7-foot bath. Painted poplar walls, a tub surround of slab slate, and a vanity of salvaged antique chestnut wood give this bath a look of refined rusticity. If your budget won't go quite that far, painted walls, large slate tiles, and distressed oak (or another wood with a pronounced grain) can be used for a similar effect if the workmanship is good. Even more important than surfacing materials are the practical comforts this room provides: an extra-deep soaking tub, double sinks and medicine chests, and separate glass-enclosed compartments for the toilet and shower.

Above: *Glass doors filter light from the single window (reflected in the shower door) into the toilet and shower cubicles. In a witty design gesture, the shower compartment has a clear glass door with a frosted glass transom, while the toilet compartment features a frosted glass door with a clear glass transom.*

Left: *Rustic but luxurious materials, mostly slate slabs and antique chestnut wood planks, offer subtle colors and textures that enhance this bath's quiet atmosphere.*

Opposite: *A modern, minimalist aesthetic invokes this bath in a vintage beach cottage with a feeling that's far from the usual nostalgic treatment given this type of room. Walls are painted poplar wood; the tub surround is slab slate.* Architect: Stuart Disston, AIA, Austin Patterson Disston Architects.

Echoes of the Far East infuse these two very different baths. The result is a sense of poise and peacefulness that makes them the perfect refuge. In one, a rigorously symmetrical layout and a host of subtly elegant details create the air of quiet dignity. In the other, a masterpiece of a ceiling leads the design, evoking an exotic island hideaway. Both these rooms have refused the obviously glamorous moves often used to create opulent baths. But they're still clearly aristocratic. The vanities, for example, are masterpieces of modern simplicity, flawlessly designed and engineered. Walls in fine marble or plaster impart traditional elegance with their heavy, ornate trim molding. The freestanding tubs, most often associated with traditional style, have transcended their origins (especially the tub with the flat bottom rather than claw feet). As almost sculptural elements, these tubs make bathing the restoring ritual it can be. There's not a hint of gilding here, but for discerning homeowners, the elegant message comes through.

Right: *A simple yet sublimely luxurious hideaway, this bath seems designed for contemplation and renewal. An exotic vaulted ceiling recalls village houses in the South Seas; other tropical, colonial influences are also apparent. In this context, the freestanding tub can be seen for its sculptural beauty.*

Opposite: *Asian elements of style converge to create this dignified eclectic master bath. An enviable symmetrical balance has been achieved here; even the doors align to create a regal pathway to the opulent bed. A claw-foot tub takes pride of place in the foreground; identical vanity sinks flank the doorway. Every detail has been thought through.*

THIS LITTLE BATH packs a powerful amount of high design appeal into a relatively small space. If you've despaired of transforming your standard-size bathroom into a dramatic design statement, here's proof it can be done. A soothing scheme of Nile green and white visually expands and freshens the space, while a mix of metals adds the necessary spark. Unlike many rooms that reveal everything at once, this deftly done little bath demands some discovering. The brass trim around the tile, for example, isn't just good-looking: It unobtrusively provides all the places to prop bath supplies, candles, or toys anyone could ever want, without adding bulky cabinets. The conventional toilet tank is partly hidden by the granite slab vanity, and the shower curtain bar is camouflaged by an overhead beam. The burnished metal sink bowl makes a dramatic design statement without taking up a lot of space, an ideal this whole room fulfills with pizzazz.

Left: *Brand new yet timelessly styled, this burnished metal sink bowl rests completely on top of the granite slab vanity shelf. The savvily sited toilet tissue holder is accessible but not right out in view, as in most baths.*

Opposite: *Nile green mosaic tiles make a see-worthy spa of this small bath. The tiles are topped with an L-shape brass trim that gives a sparkling finish and provides virtually unlimited shelf space for bath supplies, anywhere around the room.*

THIS TRANSITIONAL-STYLE BATH proves the timeless appeal of an architectural design with "good bones," followed through with quality materials and execution. It's difficult to decide what's most eye-catching in this space: the dramatic oversize skylight, the masterful vanity curving onto a second wall, or the frivolously pretty candle sconce contrasting with so much geometry. All these elements, large and small, work and look well together. The space offers an array of ideas worth considering for your bath, whatever its size. Your vanity may not be a serpentine affair, but it should still include as many open/display and closed/private storage compartments as space allows and be rendered in the nicest material your budget will accommodate. Your shower stall may be smaller, but adding a built-in bench (perhaps a pull-down model if space is really tight) is a sensible convenience. And whatever your budget or style, you can't do better for accessories than a few fresh blooms and candles!

Above: *A sleekly simple shower stall, generous in size, features the added comfort of a built-in seat. The frameless glass door enhances the simple sculptural effect of the compartment's design.*

Right: *A masterfully designed vanity includes all the storage, both open and closed, any user would ever need, all wrapped up in a handsome piece of furniture. Echoing the curved motif throughout the room, the vanity swerves gently to avoid a sharp right angle as it flows onto an adjacent wall. Cool metal pulls enhance the vanity's Art Deco–inspired good looks.*

Opposite: *This bath's design is unusually dynamic thanks to the series of repeated curves and squares balancing one another. Against this array of forthright shapes, the irrepressibly curly wall sconce, complete with real candles, lends an eye-catching, romantic contrast.* Designer: Gabriella Toro, Cippananda Interior Design.

IF YOU CRAVE a timelessly beautiful look for your bath, borrow some special effects from this sophisticated yet soothing space. Fine wood cabinets wear a subtle washed finish that high-lights the traditional raised-panel design. In addition to an abundance of storage cabinets and drawers, the handsome vanity includes a tambour-doored personal appliance garage at countertop level. Stone and tumbled marble tiles frame the space with classic, understated elegance. The tiles' rough, matte texture contrasts nicely with the array of smooth, shining glass and mirror surfaces, but this design goes one step further. Key areas of glass are frosted or swirled, giving them textures of their own and providing a perfect bridge between tradi-tional and modern elements. The swirled-glass countertop that runs the length of the vanity is particularly impressive, creating a brilliant reference to flowing water. It's in these refer-ences to nature that modern and traditional design elements come together most elegantly.

Left: *Precisely frosted glass bordered by clear glass on these French doors echoes the raised-panel design of the vanity cabinets. While the cabinets are traditional and the doors are contemporary, the repeated design motif acts as a bridge to create harmony in the space.*

Right: *Swirling "combed" glass suggesting the pattern of waves transforms this shower stall into a work of art. Inside, tumbled marble tiles with a weathered look and a classic "sunflower" showerhead add to the calming, timeless effect.*

Bathing is a unique experience in these three settings that take creative design to the next level. Soft, neutral tones straight from nature create a soothing ambience, while tub and shower designs recall the most elemental, timeless human experience with water. While some would label these bathrooms contemporary style because of their bold simplicity, there's no denying the subtle influences from ancient Eastern cultures that infuse these designs with depth. The Asian-inspired vanity in one room works nicely with the sculptural, modern wood side table, while the thick, white stucco walls of another evoke ancient desert cultures from Egypt to Mexico. Whether or not you spring for a totally custom, unique design like one of these, you can easily incorporate ideas from these rooms. The prescription is simple: timeless Asian, Middle Eastern, and South American motifs and materials; lots of white or other light, neutral tones; and stone, wood, wicker, and other natural materials. Mix well, and relax!

Above: *Rough-hewn limestone panels this unique shower for an enchanting, grotto-like atmosphere that's truly timeless. The design isn't just eye-catching, however; it cleverly provides ledges for seating and shelves for bath supplies—or a humidity-loving plant.*

Left: *Eye-pleasing curves in the vaulted ceiling of this bathing nook are echoed in the smooth, rounded form of the soaking tub. The rim of the tub is wide enough to hold bath supplies, so nothing mars the pristine, sensuous forms of the room.*

Opposite: *A truly extraordinary tub with a surround of rough-hewn stone is one amazing focal point in this bath. A wall of white limestone and an Asian-inspired vanity of wood and bamboo also celebrate the captivating tones and textures of natural materials.*

A BATH CLEARLY INSPIRED BY the timeless Chinese aesthetic is dramatic, restrained, exciting, and simple—all at the same time. Cinnabar, the rich red color of Chinese lacquer, takes center stage on a masterfully designed vanity and is balanced by strong planes of black and white throughout the room. One design element that contributes to the solid sense of dignity in this space is a series of grids: small on the authentic Asian shoji screen, midsize on the cabinet's mullions, and large on the floor tiles and transom-height windows. Contrasting this rather austere geometry, Chinese scenes of nature and a vase filled with exuberant sprays of white orchids create a soothing balance. Where a Western modern design based on red, white, and black would most likely be a sharper look, this design reveals its Asian sensibilities with a richer, more subtle color scheme that also includes a floor interestingly mottled in blues and greens and a variety of jade green accents.

Right: *An assortment of Chinese artifacts brings out additional accent colors of jade and celadon green as well as adding an elegant extra touch to underscore the room's theme.*

Opposite: *Cinnabar makes this massive double vanity an especially striking focal point. The vanity includes a shared upper cabinet with a frosted glass door reminiscent of classic Asian shoji screens. One such actual screen is used as an accent piece in the spacious room.* **Manufacturer: Wood-Mode.**

Above: *Even small details are handled perfectly to create a special ambience in this bath. The silvery shark's-tooth drawer and cabinet pulls add a handsome jewelry touch; carved bun feet in ebony give the vanity a freestanding-furniture look.*

THE SIMPLICITY of this room is not one of blandness. Rather, it recalls the willingly endured simplicity that evokes the freedom of an adventurous outdoor life in faraway climes. Plain white fixtures, quiet cotton fabrics, and the simplest of wood accessories do the job nicely, but it's easy to see there's more to this room than the bare basics. Those plain white fixtures, for example, get a lift from brightly gleaming fittings instead of the expected brushed finish models. For natural richness, weathered, softly colored brick tiles laid in a herringbone pattern evoke the feeling of an ancient courtyard. Trays and baskets, storage solutions since the earliest times, still serve nicely today in a nearby shelving unit. Whether you live in a city loft or a country cottage, there's something to like about a style that requires so little for function and style. This is a romantic look that has nothing to do with balloon shades and everything to do with a free-spirited approach to everyday life.

Left: *Berber striped cloth defines the rustic shower and clothes hamper; naturally finished wood creates a simple yet handsome triptych mirror and towel rack. These unassuming elements reach into our nomadic past for timeless inspiration.*

Opposite: *A member of the French Foreign Legion might have stolen a few hours of respite in this rustic yet comfortable bath. Thoughtful touches include a small stool to keep the news from home dry, a nearby rack for towels, and an amply sized bath tray to hold a travel journal and a cool drink.*

Opposite: *Opulently decorated, this claw-foot tub makes a dramatic focal point that stands up to the strong architecture of the space. A soft, appealing blend of tones makes the standard-size tiles worth a second look; extra-large tiles in white give the room a spacious, calm feeling.*

Blue and white, probably the best-loved color scheme in the world, gives these transitional baths a timeless quality. In true eclectic style, they exhibit a spirited mix of architectural, fixture, and accessory styles. One bath uses both a vintage-look claw-foot bathtub and a briskly modern accessory cart in chrome and glass. The other pairs strong modern architecture with a pattern-painted claw-foot tub and nostalgic accessories. To make these rooms serene as well as fun, the owners willingly accepted the trade-off for using such a wide range of styles: sticking to a limited selection of colors. One space uses standard-size tiles in a moody mix of hues; the other uses a playful mosaic tile pattern as an accent that also makes the double-sink vanity into an artful focal point. But looks aren't everything, so these baths have also planned in practical comforts, starting with places to keep bath supplies within hand's reach of the tub.

An old-fashioned claw-foot tub, an industrial-style stainless-steel cart, a Swedish sauna-inspired slatted wood mat, and south-of-the-border window plants all work together. Each piece is a great example of its type, and the color palette is as disciplined as the mix is wild.

A crisp palette of true blue and bright white is fresh and classic at the same time. What makes it really special, however, is the use of small mosaic tiles in a mix of heavenly blues, dark and light. The mix acts as a bridge between the all-white tiles and the painted blue surfaces.

European Esprit

Transitional style may be achieved by using elements that combine both modern and traditional design signatures; for example, a traditional toile (scenic-patterned) fabric in a bold, modern color. It may also be achieved by balancing contemporary and traditional elements in eclectic fashion. In either scenario, the effect can be the best of both worlds: the free-spirited simplicity of contemporary style and the elegant warmth of traditional style. While some might think of transitional style as American, it's as likely to appear in European-inspired rooms. With so many ancient treasures near at hand yet so much that had to be replaced after World War II, Europe evolved a uniquely rich form of transitional style. That style is amply evidenced in these two baths. Open spaces decorated with only a few grand gestures, these baths are appointed with just the right mix of modern conveniences and timeless comforts. The result: quietly romantic retreats.

Left: *Floor-length draperies, a small, traditional side chair, and a tub framed in a recessed panel surround give this bath a serene look, while the modern fixtures offer up-to-date convenience.* Designer: Armitage Shanks.

Right: *A traditional claw-foot tub and generously scaled pedestal sink provide basic comforts in this bath that recalls an artist's studio. Flanking the sink, a huge loft-type window and a modern lamp perched on a freestanding chest shed ample light on the subject.* Fixtures and fittings: American Standard.

Supremely serene and elegant but never too serious, this bath illustrates eclectic style at its best. A spectacular focal point, like the beautifully carved Renaissance-style vanity, stands out all the more against a simple background of ivory stone tiles. The wicker towel basket and sculpted chair are modern, casual elements chosen for their graceful lines, so it's not surprising that they're in harmony with the more traditional elements. At the same time, they provide an irreverent note that's downright dashing. Keeping all elements in a neutral monochromatic scheme of ivory-through-brown is key to tying this wide range of hand-picked elements together. Experts recommend that, in general, the more expressive and experimental the element mix, the more conservative the color scheme should be, and vice versa. Be sure, too, that all major elements are roughly of the same quality level: In a room this simple, every item needs to be a player.

Exquisite carvings recall the splendors of the 1600s on the face of this fine vanity cabinet. A beveled-edge marble top holds more classic accessories, including a vintage six-drawer spice box that's perfect for holding jewelry or small makeup items.

Left: *A muted wash of ivory, tan, and brown unites the elements in this room, even though they're from vastly different eras and moods. A beautifully carved Renaissance-style vanity cabinet mingles with a classic modern chair from the mid-20th century and a very casual tawny basket.*

Above: *Neutral tones, masterfully deployed in a truly spectacular floor tile design, take on an extraordinary visual depth and richness. The handsome vanity with its distinctive crown is a fitting companion to the world-class floor.*

This masterful master bath indulges its owner's love affair with strong geometric patterns. A riot of stripes, triangles, and related shapes are combined and repeated in a dizzying array that creates the optical illusion of physical dimension on a flat plane and movement in an architectural space. The overall effect is not jarring, however, just tremendously energizing. The design, while fearless, stays within the bounds of comfort thanks to a soothing color scheme of neutrals: gold, brown, taupe-gray, white, and black. This strategy makes sense regardless of how opulent your bath plan may be. Of course, it doesn't hurt if you can manage a floor made of no less than five different kinds of marble, a showstopping shower stall, and a vanity as handsome and dramatic as a piece of drawing room furniture. But even if you can't quite muster these extraordinary elements, you can still aim for a winning look of restrained richness and focused energy.

Left: *Overlooking a tranquil walled garden, this tub gains extra distinction from its unique striped surround. The striped motif is carried out in towels and accents and punctuated by the chic formality of black.* Whirlpool tub: Sanijet Pipeless Whirlpool Bath. **Opposite:** *Angled showers are often inherently dramatic, but this one is clearly a cut above the rest. The meticulous decorative tile work that makes this bath's floor such a standout appears on a smaller scale in the shower.* Architect: John Brooks. Builder: Sharif & Munir Enterprises Inc. Designer: Maxine Smith, Margo Design Associates. Shower: Alumax Bath Enclosures.

Above: *A warming rack is stationed near the bidet—a continental touch that could really spoil you. Above, Art Deco wall sconces shed light on the Cézanne-inspired still life oil painting. Artwork enriches any space, and that includes the bath!*

A *SOUPÇON* of French style goes a long way to transform any bath, but in this spectacular space, the owners are completely surrounded by Parisian inspirations. Evoking something of the spirit of the Orient Express, the famed Paris-to-Constantinople luxury train made famous by Agatha Christie, this bath is glamorous, luxurious, and a bit mysterious. Art Deco–style fixtures, fittings, and accessories, all in gleaming chrome, stand out against the black, white, and mustard gold background. Special touches abound: A sunflower showerhead is the crowning glory of a tub fitting system more elaborate than a steam calliope. A tiger-stripe floor-cloth adds punch, while fine art in the French Impressionist style offers an extra dimension of elegance. With all this opulence, the space has an austere aesthetic that is quite contemporary. The cleverly designed space uses dark and warm colors to create a sense of richness, while the smooth, shiny textures balance with coolness. *C'est très chic!*

Right: *A fantastical multifaucet shower/ bath fitting, like something out of a Jules Verne novel, looks even more dramatic against a wall of gold-and-brown tortoise-shell marble inset with a band of black marble. Practical touches include a built-in marble shelf to keep bath supplies at hand.*

Opposite: *A pair of matching classic pedestal sinks with traditional cross-handle fittings would be handsome any-where, but they're especially effective in this dramatic space. A wall of black glass, inset with perfectly round chrome-framed Art Deco–style mirrors, makes a simply spec-tacular setting.*

Resource Directory

ARCHITECTS

Adirondack Design Associates
77 Riverside Drive
Saranac Lake, NY 12983
phone 518-891-5224
fax 518-891-5227
Michael Bird

**Austin Patterson
Disston Architects**
376 Pequot Ave.
Southport, CT 06490
phone 203-255-4031
fax 203-254-1390
Stuart Disston, AIA

John Brooks
6319 Windmill Circle
Dallas, TX 75252
phone 972-985-8022

Charles Cunniffe Architects
610 E. Hyman
Aspen, CO 81611
phone 970-925-5590
fax 970-925-4557
www.cunniffe.com

David Cofrances, AIA
825 Marco Pl.
Venice, CA 90291
phone 310-821-6250

Peter Cook, AIA
280 Elm St.
Southampton, NY 11968
phone 631-283-0077
fax 631-283-5960

John M. Eide, Jr.
P.O. Box 1010
Lakeville, CT 06039
phone 860-435-4771

John Kerr Associates
53A Bayham St.
London NW1 0AA ENGLAND
phone 011-44-2072-092-784
fax 011-44-2072-092-786
jkerrassoc@aol.com
John Kerr

Sidnam Petrone Gartner
136 W. 21 St.
New York, NY 10011
phone 212-366-5500
fax 212-366-6559
sidnampetr@aol.com

BUILDERS

Alpine Log Homes
118 Main
Victor, MT 59875
phone 406-642-3451

Rocky Mountain Log Homes
1883 Highway 93 S
Hamilton, MT 59840
phone 406-363-5680
fax 406-363-2109
sales@rmlh.com
www.rmlh.com

**Sharif & Munir
Enterprises Inc.**
6009 Beltline Road, Suite 200
Dallas, TX 75240
phone 972-788-1234
fax 972-702-8533
staff@sharif-munir.com
www.sharif-munir.com

DESIGNERS

Ann Morris Interiors, Ltd.
515 Madison Ave.
New York, NY 10022
phone 212-688-7564
fax 718-441-8384
annmorrisints@
worldnet.att.net
www.kitchen-design-ny.com
Ann M. Morris, CKD, CBD

Armitage Shanks
Armitage, Rugeley
Staffordshire WS15 4BT
ENGLAND
phone 011-44-1543-490-253
fax 011-44-1543-491-677
www.armitage-shanks.co.uk

Arxis Design Studio
11024 Washington Blvd.
Culver City, CA 90232
phone 310-559-6212
fax 310-559-6313
www.arxis-work.com
*Leonardo Umansky and
Ramiro Diazgranados*

Bacarella Martin Interiors
59 White Road
Shrewsbury, NJ 07702
phone 732-530-9545
fax 732-530-5591

Betsy Meyer Associates, Inc.
692 Montauk Highway
Water Mill, NY 11976
phone 631-726-6428
fax 631-726-6453
Betsy Meyer, CKD, CBD

John A. Buscarello, ASID
27 W. 20th St.
New York, NY 10011
phone 212-691-5881
fax 212-691-5916

Lori W. Carroll, ASID
1200 N. El Dorado Pl.
Suite B200
Tucson, AZ 85715
phone 520-886-3443, x1
fax 520-772-8385
lori@interlinedesign.com
www.loricarroll.com

Esther Chopp
21 Marshall Drive
Edison, NJ 08817
phone 732-572-7977
fax 732-572-2099

Cippananda Interior Design
521 Strand St.
Santa Monica, CA 90405
phone 310-396-1515
fax 310-396-8315
Gabriella Toro

Custom Kitchens by
John Wilkins Inc.
6624 Telegraph Ave.
Oakland, CA 94609
phone 510-843-3600
fax 510-848-0545
custkit@dnai.com
www.customkitchen.net
Joy Wilkins

Decorating Den Interiors
19100 Montgomery Village
Montgomery Village, MD
20886
phone 800-DEC-DENS
www.decoratingden.com
Lisa Landry

Design for Sale
23679 Calabasas Road
Suite 347
Calabasas, CA 91302
phone 818-888-6094
fax 818-888-6095
leshay@msn.com
www.designforsale.com
Andrea LeShay

Fairhaven Design
3 E. Front St.
Red Bank, NJ 07701
phone 732-842-1400
fax 732-842-3723

JJ Interiors
P.O. Box 5130
Chapel Hill, NC 27514
phone 919-542-1447
Janine Jordan, CKD, IIDA, IDS

Jackie Naylor Interiors
4287 Glengary Drive
Atlanta, GA 30342
phone 404-814-1973
fax 404-814-9030

Jeanne Leonard Interiors, Inc.
10 Beach Road
Westhampton Beach, NY 11978
Jeanne Leonard

John Robert Wiltgen
Design, Inc.
70 W. Hubbard
Chicago, IL 60610
phone 312-744-1151
John Robert Wiltgen

Kitchen Dimensions
150 S. St. Francis
Santa Fe, NM 87501
phone 505-986-8820
fax 505-986-5888

The Kitchen Specialist, Inc.
3407 University Drive
Durham, NC 27707
phone 919-490-4922
fax 919-286-4922
maryliebhold@
thekitchenspecialist.com
Mary T. Liebhold, CKD

Kitchen Studio
5200 Eubank Blvd. NE
Albuquerque, NM 87111
phone 505-294-6767
fax 505-294-6763
kitstu5200@aol.com
www.kitchenstudioabq.com
*Joe McDermott and
Diane Wandmaker, CKD*

Kitchens by Kleweno
4034 Broadway
Kansas City, MO 64111
phone 816-531-3968
fax 816-531-8566
Randy Sisk

Kitchens by Wieland, Inc.
4210 Tilghman St.
Allentown, PA 18104
phone 610-395-2074
fax 610-395-4762
wiel-kit-bath@fast.net
www.kitchensbywieland.com
Robert L. Wieland, CKD, CBD

Kohler
Kohler, WI 53044
phone 920-457-4441
fax 920-459-1656
www.kohlerco.com

Rebecca Gullion Lindquist,
CKD, CBD
926 E. 4th St.
Duluth, MN 55805
phone 218-728-5171
fax 218-728-5173
lindco@cpinternet.com
www.lindquistandcompany.com

Margo Design Associates
18352 Dallas Parkway
Suite 13b
PMB544, Dallas, TX 75287
phone 972-713-0600
Maxine Smith

Miner Details
31 Muscogee Ave. NW
Atlanta, GA 30305
phone 404-262-9719
Jay Miner

MK Designs
6835 Ravine Court
Newcastle, CA 95658
phone 916-663-3412
fax 916-663-0150
mkdesigns@webdba.com
*Molly Korb, CKD, CBD, and
Linda Panattoni*

Monson Interior Design, Inc.
275 Market St., Suite 292
Minneapolis, MN 55405
phone 612-338-0665
fax 612-338-0855
monson@mail.visi.com
*Lynn Monson, ASID, CKD,
CBD, CID*

National Kitchen & Bath
Association (NKBA)
687 Willow Grove St.
Hackettstown, NJ 07840
phone 800-843-6522

Riverside Custom Design
20956 Mack Ave.
Grosse Pointe Woods, MI
48236
phone 313-886-3188
fax 313-886-3623
riverside@ameritech.net
www.riversidecustom.com
Gene Pindzia

Rogers-Ford, L.C.
2616 Thomas Ave.
Dallas, TX 75204
phone 214-871-9388
fax 214-871-3155
info@rogers-ford.com

Rutt of Atlanta
351 Peachtree Hills Ave.
Suite 413
Atlanta, GA 30305
phone 404-264-9698
fax 404-264-0346
www.rutt1.com
Jere Bowden, CKD, and
Emmye Otto, CKD

Sandra Steiner-Houck,
CKD, Inc.
Three Kacey Court, Suite 201
Mechanicsburg, PA 17055
phone 717-591-0562
fax 717-591-0563
Sandra Steiner-Houck, CKD

Showcase Kitchens and
Baths, Inc.
8122-B S. Lewis
Tulsa, OK 74137
phone 918-299-4232
fax 918-299-4272
www.kitchenandbathshowcase.
com
Sally Ann Sullivan, CKD

Sieger Design
Schloss Harkotten
D-4414 Sassenberg 2
GERMANY
phone 011-49-5426-3298
fax 011-49-5426-3875
Dieter Sieger

Bil Taylor
178 E. Broadway
Tucson, AZ 85701
phone 520-792-9544
fax 520-792-2029
wtaylor282@aol.com

Trout Studios
5880 Blackwelder
Culver City, CA 90232
phone 310-202-8868
fax 310-202-8896
talk@troutstudios.com
www.troutstudios.com
Sallie Trout

Walker Zanger
13190 Telfair Ave.
Sylmar, CA 91342
phone 818-504-0235
fax 818-252-4103
kbernard@walkerzanger.com
www.walkerzanger.com
Kim Bernard, ASID

Zimmerman Design Group
7707 Harwood Ave.
Milwaukee, WI 53213
phone 414-476-9500
fax 414-476-8582
www.zdg.com
Robert E. Lewcock, ASID

MANUFACTURERS
Alchemy Glass & Light
3143 S. La Cienega Blvd.
Los Angeles, CA 90016
phone 310-836-8631
fax 310-836-8695
info@alchemy-glass.com
www.alchemy-glass.com

Alsons
42 Union St.
Hillsdale, MI 49242
phone 517-439-1411
fax 517-439-9644
www.alsons.com

Alumax Bath Enclosures
1617 N. Washington
Magnolia, AR 71753
phone 870-234-4260
fax 870-234-3181
alumaxlt@ipa.net
www.alumag.com

American Standard
One Centennial Plaza
P.O. Box 6820
Piscataway, NJ 08855
phone 732-980-3000
www.americanstandard-us.com

Andersen Windows, Inc.
100 4th Ave. N
Bayport, MN 55003-1096
phone 800-426-4261
www.andersenwindows.com

Ann Sacks Tile & Stone
8120 N.E. 33rd Drive
Portland, OR 97211
phone 503-281-7751

AquaDreams Ltd.
8606-A Melrose Ave.
Los Angeles, CA 90069
phone 310-657-3131
fax 310-657-3107
nadia@aquadreamsinc.com
www.aquadreamsltd.com

Aqua Glass
Industrial Park, P.O. Box 412
Adamsville, TN 38310
phone 901-632-2501
www.aquaglass.com

Briggs Plumbing Products, Inc.
1720 E. Main St.
Duncan, SC 29334
phone 864-433-1454
fax 864-433-9443
www.briggsplumbing.com

Broan
P.O. Box 140, 926 W. State St.
Hartford, WI 53027
phone 800-548-0790
fax 262-673-8709
www.broan.com

Corning
One Riverfront Plaza
Corning, NY 14831
phone 607-974-9000
www.corning.com

Crestwood
601 E. Water Well Road
Salina, KS 67401
phone 800-235-2618
fax 785-827-0084
www.crestwood-inc.com

Decorá
One MasterBrand
Cabinets Drive
Jasper, IN 47546
phone 812-482-2527
fax 812-634-2850
info@masterbrandcabinets.
com
www.decoracabinets.com

Dornbracht USA
1750 Breckinridge Parkway
Suite 510
Duluth, GA 30096
phone 770-564-3599
fax 800-899-8527
info@dornbracht.com
www.dornbracht.com

Draper–DBS, Inc.
1803 N. 5th St.
Perkasie, PA 18944
phone 215-453-7661
fax 215-453-7669
www.draperdbs.com

DuPont Corian
P.O. Box 80012
Wilmington, DE 19880-0702
phone 800-4-CORIAN
www.corian.com

Easco
Three Industrial Drive
Vernon, NJ 07462
phone 973-209-4141
fax 973-209-7621

FSC Wallcoverings
79 Madison Ave.
New York, NY 10016
phone 212-213-7909
fax 212-213-7640
bskelly@fsco.com
www.villagehome.com

F. Schumacher & Co.
79 Madison Ave.
New York, NY 10016
www.fsco.com

Geberit Manufacturing, Inc.
1100 Boone Drive
Michigan City, IN 46360
phone 800-225-7217
fax 219-872-8003
www.us.geberit.com

Grohe
241 Covington Drive
Bloomingdale, IL 60108
phone 630-582-7711
fax 630-582-7722
info@groheamerica.com
www.grohe.com

Hallmark
4851 S. Warehouse Road
Salt Lake City, UT 84118
phone 801-966-0562
fax 201-966-8114
www.hallmarkcabinet.com

Hansgrohe
Auestr. 5-9
77761 Schiltach GERMANY
phone 011-49-7836-51-0
fax 011-49-7836-51-1300
www.hansgrohe.com

Heritage Custom Kitchens
215 Diller Ave.
New Holland, PA 17557
phone 717-354-4011
fax 717-355-0169
www.hck.com

Ideal Standard
The Bathroom Works
National Ave.
Kingston Upon Hull HU5 4HS
ENGLAND
phone 011-44-1482-346-461
fax 011-44-1482-445-886
www.ideal-standard.co.uk

Indus Ceramica
Via Radici In Piano 558
Sassuolo, Modena 41049 ITALY
phone 011-39-059-571-777
fax 011-39-059-571-009

Jacuzzi Whirlpool Bath
2121 N. California Blvd.
Walnut Creek, CA 94596
phone 800-288-4002
fax 925-256-1749
info@jacuzzi.com
www.jacuzzi.com

Junckers
Units 3–5 Wheaton Court
Commercial Centre/
Wheaton Road
Witham, Essex CM8 3UJ
ENGLAND
phone 011-44-1376-517-512

Kohler
*Please see Designers list for
contact information.*

Lee Bays Concrete
4945 E. Fairmount
Tucson, AZ 85712
phone 520-327-1759

Lighting by Leader
1110 Close Ave.
Bronx, NY 10472

Maax
600 Cameron
Sainte-Marie, QE G6E 1B2
CANADA
phone 800-463-6229
fax 418-387-3507

Mannington
P.O. Box 30, Route 45
Mannington Mills Road
Salem, NJ 08079-0030
phone 856-935-3000
fax 856-339-5948
www.mannington.com

Milling Road
329 N. Hamilton St.
High Point, NC 27260
phone 800-592-2537

Nessen Lighting
420 Railroad Way
Mamaroneck, NY 10543
phone 914-698-7799
fax 914-698-5577
www.nessenlighting.com

Newport Brass
3131 S. Standard Ave.
Santa Ana, CA 92705
phone 714-436-0805
fax 714-436-0806

Ottoman Treasures
801 S. Highland St.
Mount Dora, FL 32757
phone 352-383-6286
fax 352-383-6317
www.ottomantreasure.com
ottoman@sundial.net

Rutt Custom Cabinetry
1564 Main St., P.O. Box 129
Goodville, PA 17528
phone 800-220-RUTT
www.rutt.net

Rutt of Atlanta
*Please see Designers list for
contact information.*

**Sanijet Pipeless
Whirlpool Bath**
1461 S. Beltline Road
Coppell, TX 75019
phone 877-934-0477
fax 877-834-0477
sales@sanijet.com
www.sanijet.com

Seabrook Wallcoverings, Inc.
1325 Farmville Road
Memphis, TN 38122
phone 800-238-9152
www.seabrookwallcoverings.
com

Sottini
The Bathroom Works
National Ave.
Kingston Upon Hull HU5 4HS
ENGLAND
phone 011-44-1482-449-513
fax 011-44-1482-445-886
www.sottini.co.uk

StarMark Cabinetry, Inc.
600 E. 48th St. N
Sioux Falls, SD 57104
phone 800-594-9444
fax 605-336-5574
inquire@starmarkcabinetry.
com
www.starmarkcabinetry.com

Steamist
275 Veterans Blvd.
Rutherford, NJ 07070
phone 201-933-0700
fax 201-933-0746
steamist@worldnet.att.net
www.steamistco.com

Stone Source
215 Park Ave. S
New York, NY 10003
phone 212-979-6400

Sylvan Designs, Inc.
8921 Quartz Ave.
Northridge, CA
phone 818-998-6868
fax 818-998-7241
www.sylvandesigns.com

Tower Ceramics
91 Parkway
Camden Town, London
NW1 7PP ENGLAND
phone 011-44-20-7485-7192

Trajet
phone 800-872-5381
trajet@radiks.net
www.trajet.com

Timothy Haglund Studio
112 E. Mineral St.
Milwaukee, WI 53204
phone 414-672-7007
fax 414-672-1193

Trout Studios
*Please see Designers list for
contact information.*

UltraCraft
6163 Old 421 Road
Liberty, NC 27298
phone 336-622-4281
fax 336-622-3474
www.ultracraft.com

Vola
Unit 12/Ampthill Business Park,
Ampthill
Bedford, Bedfordshire MK
452QW
phone 011-44-1525-841-155

Walker Zanger
*Please see Designers list for
contact information.*

Waterworks
191 N.E. 40th St., Suite 101
Miami, FL 33137
phone 305-573-5943
fax 305-573-1744

Wilsonart
phone 800-433-3222

Wm Ohs, Inc.
5095 Peoria St.
Denver, CO 80239
phone 303-371-6550
fax 303-371-6601
www.wmohs.com

Wood-Mode
One 2nd St.
Kreamer, PA 17833
phone 570-374-2711
fax 570-372-1422
www.wood-mode.com

York Wallcoverings
750 Linden Ave.
York, PA 17405
phone 800-375-YORK
fax 717-854-9753
ad@yorkwall.com

Yorktowne Cabinets
P.O. Box 231
Red Lion, PA 17356-0231
phone 800-777-0065
fax 717-244-5168
cabinets@yorktwn.com
www.yorktowneinc.com

PHOTOGRAPHERS
Abode Interiors UK
Albion Court, One Pierce St.
Macclesfield, Cheshire
SK11 6ER ENGLAND
phone 011-44-1625-500-070
fax 011-44-1625-500-910

Ray Allbright
phone 520-318-4121

Tom Bonner
1201 Abbot Kinney Blvd.
Venice, CA 90291
phone 310-396-7125
fax 310-396-4792

Jim Brandenburg
5842 Moose Lake Road
Ely, MN 55731
phone 218-365-5105

Crofoot Photography
1001 Washington Ave. S
Minneapolis, MN 55415
phone 612-339-9191
fax 612-339-9009
pamela@crofootphoto.com
www.crofootphoto.com

D² Studios
1526 Edison St.
Dallas, TX 75207
phone 214-746-6336
fax 214-746-6338
Doug Davis

David Duncan Livingston
Photography
1036 Erica Road
Mill Valley, CA 94941
phone 415-383-0898
fax 415-383-0897
ddl@davidduncanlivingston.
com
www.davidduncanlivingston.
com

Colleen Duffley
3303 Lee Parkway
Dallas, TX 75219
phone 214-520-9675

Phillip H. Ennis
426 Pennsylvania Ave.
Freeport, NY 11520
phone 516-379-4276

Nancy Hill
210 Mamanasco Road
Ridgefield, CT 06877
203-431-7655

In Focus Associates
251 W. 92nd St.
New York, NY 10025
phone 212-593-5100
fax 212-799-7942
Jeff McNamara

The Interior Archive Ltd.
401 Fulham Road
London SW6 1EB ENGLAND
phone 011-44-1713-700-595
fax 011-44-1819-602-695

Jeff Frey and Associates
405 E. Superior St.
Duluth, MN 55802
phone 218-722-6630
fax 218-722-8425

Jeff Garland Photography
4083 Utica Road
Sterling Heights, MI 48313
phone 810-264-4441
fax 810-268-3289
jgphoto@earthlink.net

Jeff Heatley Photography
P.O. Box 1188
Mattituck, NY 11952
phone 631-287-0366

Vincent Lisanti
330 Clinton Ave.
Dobbs Ferry, NY 10522
phone 914-693-5273
104507.130@compuserve.com

Melabee M. Miller
29 Beechwood Pl.
Hillside, NJ 07205
phone 908-527-9121
fax 902-527-0242
mmiller95@aol.com

Emily Minton
P.O. Box 77462
Atlanta, GA 30357-1462
phone 404-355-8818

Michael Moran
371 Broadway
New York, NY 10013
phone 212-334-4543
fax 212-334-3854

Bradley Olman
145 Oakland St.
Red Bank, NJ 07701

Photofields
36W830 Stonebridge Lane
St. Charles, IL 60175
phone 630-587-5530

Jerry Rabinowitz
phone 561-870-6300
fax 561-852-4636
jerry@jrabinowitz.com
www.jrabinowitz.com

Derek Rath
4044 Moore St.
Los Angeles, CA 90066
phone 310-305-1342
rathd@earthlink.net

Real Images
3003 Mulberry St.
Marietta, GA 30066
phone 678-290-7800
fax 678-290-7722
realimages1@mindspring.com
John Umberger

Samu Studios
P.O. Box 165
Bay Port, NY 11705
phone 212-754-0415
www.samustudios.com

Brad Simmons
870 Craintown Road
Perryville, KY 40468
phone 859-332-8400

Beth Singer
25741 River Drive
Franklin, MI 48025
phone 248-626-4860
fax 248-932-3496

Tim Street-Porter
2074 Watsonia Terrace
Los Angeles, CA 90068
phone 323-874-4278

Robert Thien
2432 Sunset Drive
Atlanta, GA 30345
phone 404-486-9813

Brian Vanden Brink
39 Curtis Ave.
Camden, ME 04843
phone 207-236-4035

VIEW Pictures
14 The Dove Centre
109 Bartholomew Road
London NW5 2BJ ENGLAND
phone 020-7284-2928
fax 020-7284-3617
info@viewpictures.co.uk
www.viewpictures.co.uk
Chris Gascoigne

Maria Antonia Viteri
1702 E. 4th St.
Los Angeles, CA 90033
phone 323-267-4332

William Lesch Photography
426 S. Otero
Tucson, AZ 85701
phone 520-622-6693
coolie@theriver.com

Hub Willson
1321 N. 15th St.
Allentown, PA 18102-1068
phone 610-434-2178
fax 610-434-4185

Front cover: **Samu Studios**

Back cover: **Sottini**

Abode Interiors UK: 118, 130, 131, 136, 162, 163, 250, 251, 272, 273; **Courtesy of Alpine Log Homes/Dann Coffey Photography:** 70; **Courtesy of Andersen® Windows, Inc.:** 29, 235; **Ann Morris Interiors, Ltd./Oleg March Photography:** 41; **AquaDreams Ltd.:** 45 (left); **Armitage Shanks:** Contents, 228, 274; **Arxis Design Studio/Maria Antonia Viteri:** 171; **Austin Patterson Disston Architects/Jeff McNamara c/o In Focus Associates:** 256, 257; **Tony Berardi/Photofields:** 266; **Betsy Meyer Associates, Inc./Peter Ledwith Photography:** 134, 135; **Briggs Plumbing Products, Inc.:** 32 (top); **Carmichael Lynch:** Crofoot Photography: 21, 153, 240, 241, 275; Henke Studio: 45 (right); **Lori W. Carroll, ASID/William Lesch Photography:** 44 (top), 168, 169; **Charles Cunniffe Architects:** David O. Marlow Photography:104, 105; Steve Mundinger Photography: 117; **Cippananda Interior Design/Derek Rath:** 208, 209, 262, 263; **Custom Kitchens by John Wilkins Inc./Dennis Hartelius Photography:** 164, 165; **Daniel Hopwood Studio/Nick Carter Photography:** 216, 217; **David Duncan Livingston Photography:** 6, 8 (bottom), 24, 116, 151, 156, 157, 176, 177, 192, 193, 206, 207, 223, 238, 239, 254, 264, 265; **Decorá:** 236; **Decorating Den Interiors/Lisa Landry, Designer:** 186, 187; **Design for Sale/Jeff Heatley Photography:** 128, 129; **Dornbracht USA:** 38; **Elaine Siegel Associates:** 268, 269; **Wood-Mode:** 9, 55; **Phillip H. Ennis:** 5; Samuel Botero & Associates: 114, 115; Robert deCarlo: 179; Stephen & Gail Huberman: 72, 73, 82, 83 90, 91; **IDT/Stuart Narofsky, Architect:** 227; **Kemp-Simmons:** 93; **Charles Krewson:** 178; **M&S Associates:** 232, 233; **SHR Designs:** 16; **Stevens & Smith:** 59; **FSC Wallcoverings:** 92; **Chris Gascoigne/VIEW Pictures:** Contents, 198, 199, 210, 211; **Geberit Manufacturing, Inc./McHale & Koepke Communications:** 212, 213; **Heritage Custom Kitchens:** 142; **Nancy Hill:** Cernan Builders; 78, 79; Deborah T. Lipner Interiors, Ltd.: 244; Diana Sawicki Interior: 245; **Ideal Standard:** 229; **The Interior Archive Ltd.:** Ken Hayden: 218, 219; Simon Upton Photography: 110, 270, 271; Fritz van der Schulenburg Photography: 119, 138, 139, 204, 205, 280, 281; **Jackie Naylor Interiors/Robert Thien:** 196, 197; **Jacuzzi Whirlpool Bath/Mark Boisclair Photography:** 60; **JJ Interiors:** Vincent Lisanti: 94, 95; **John Robert Wiltgen Design, Inc./Steve Hall at Hedrich Blessing:** 146; **Kat Interiors Group Inc.:** 53 (top); **Kitchen Dimensions:** 76; **Kitchen Studio/Jerry Rabinowitz:** 8 (top), 71 (top); **Kitchens and Baths by Lynn, Inc.:** 27; **Kitchens by Wieland, Inc./Hub Willson:** 180, 181; **Kohler:** 47, 52, 172, 194, 195, 221; Jim Dase: 155; Charles Gandy & Bill Peace: 158, 159; Cynthia Leibrock: 34, 220; Robert E. Lewcock, ASID: 246, 247; Vonda Myers Tomlinson: 77; **Ann Sacks Tile & Stone:** 32 (bottom), 40; Jean Sedor: 68 (top); **Lindquist and Co./Jeff Frey & Associates:** 61, 88, 89; **Mannington:** 57; **Melabee M. Miller:** 33, 51, 80, 81, 137, 200, 201; **Monson Interior Design, Inc./Jim Brandenburg:** 48; **National Kitchen & Bath Association:** Peter Leach Photography: 237; David Duncan Livingston Photography: 67; **Novita Communications:** Eurotiles/Casa D'Europa Series: 71 (bottom); Gardenia Orchidea/Versace Series: 69; Mutina/Scorzati Series: 234; **Bradley Olman:** 31, 86, 87, 96, 97, 120, 121, 132, 133, 147, 255; **Riverside Custom Design/Jeff Garland Photography:** 160, 161; **Courtesy of Rocky Mountain Log Homes:** 98, 99, 145, 253; **Roger Wade Photography:** 252; **Rogers-Ford, L.C.:** Colleen Duffley: Contents, 106, 107; Emily Minton: 144; **Rutt of Atlanta/John Umberger c/o Real Images:** 46, 54, 74, 75, 143; **Samu Studios:** 14, 23, 112, 113, 248, 249; **Sanijet Pipeless Whirlpool Bath:** 278; **Seabrook Wallcoverings, Inc.:** 11, 44 (bottom); **Showcase Kitchens & Baths, Inc./Wm Ohs, Inc.:** 7; **Sidnam Petrone Gartner:** Langdon Clay/Andrew Garn Photography: 214, 215; Michael Moran: 174, 175, 242, 243; **Brad Simmons:** 84, 85, 100, 101, 102, 103, 108, 109, 124, 125; **Beth Singer:** 222; **Draper-DBS, Inc.:** 126, 127; **Sottini:** Contents, 26, 36, 50, 63, 111, 150, 170, 173, 188, 189; **StarMark Cabinetry, Inc.:** 66; **Tim Street-Porter:** 15, 43, 49, 122, 123, 140, 141, 148, 149, 166, 167, 182, 183, 184, 185, 224, 225, 226, 258, 259, 260, 261, 266, 267, 276, 277; **Taylor Design/Ray Allbright:** 190; **Trout Studios:** 53 (center & bottom), 202, 279; **Tom Bonner Photography:** Contents, 154, 203; **Brian Vanden Brink:** 18, 37, 230, 231; **Walker Zanger:** 13, 58, 191; **West One Bathrooms Limited:** 10; **York Wallcoverings:** Carey Lind Design Studio: 25; **Yorktowne Cabinets:** 68 (bottom).